Outlooks From a New Standpoint by Ernest Belfort Bax
Prism Key Press | www.prismkeypress.com

Outlooks From a New Standpoint

Ernest Belfort Bax

Contents

Preface...7

I...10
1. The Orator of the Human Race...................................10
2. The Decay of Pagan Thought.....................................45

II..70
3. Liberalism vs. Socialism..70
4. The Curse of Law...91
5. A Socialists' Notes on Practical Ethics.....................108
6. The Economical Basis of History..............................124
7. Individual Rights Under Socialism............................140
8. Marriage 147

III..157
9. Courage..157
10. The Practical Significance of Philosophy................173
11. Note on "Now"...190

Preface

THE present volume consists of various pieces on a somewhat wide range of subjects, but all of them having, as I believe, a common bearing. Some of them have never been published before, while others which have appeared have been largely re-written. The first part of the volume is taken up with two historical essays. The one on Anacharsis Clootz is based mainly on the exhaustive Life of Clootz, by Georges Avenel, a most remarkable contribution toward the inner history of the French Revolution, which, so far as I am aware, has never before been noticed in this country. The second part contains a collection of papers all bearing more or less directly upon Socialism, while the third part is devoted to three philosophical papers.

The inner steady break-up of the fabric of bourgeois civilisation becomes more noticeable year by year. The economic side of this cell apse, as exemplified in the unceasing labour-struggle – the absorbing topic of interest in all circles – is already beginning to directly modify political conditions. The decisive question in all elections now is the labour question. If politics has to desert its old party ties, and give itself the semblance of a social or labour content, not less so has religion. The Christian churches, their old speculative content dead and explained away, take to advocating social reforms, or nostrums, as the case may be, in the name of "true Christianity." That remarkable and protean ignis fatuus, "true Christianity," is now engaged in putting off the "old Adam" of personal holiness, spiritual regeneration, and preparation for another world, and taking to schemes for " ameliorating the condition of the masses," etc. Again, the present form of the institution of marriage has received some severe blows of late. The safety-valve (from the point of view of conventional marriage) of free divorce, recently opened in most continental countries, having been religiously sat upon by the English bourgeois, we may reasonably hope that in Britain the principle by which the clumsy mechanical compulsion of law intrudes itself into the purely personal relations of life will first receive its decisive death-blow.

The current popularity of Utopian romances, hailed with such joy by some, is not, perhaps, a very edifying sign. It indicates a demand for miracles, on the son of which, unfortunately, the quack and the impostor readily flourish. For it would be nothing less than a miracle for any human being to describe in prophetic vision the society of the future. What is effected in Utopian socialist writings is merely a travesty of the society of the present, or of the past. We can define, that is, lay down, in the abstract, the general principles on which the society of the future will be based, but we cannot describe, that is, picture, in the concrete, any state of society of which the world has had no experience. For into the reality of a society, even in its broader details, there enters a large element of contingency, of alogicality, of unreason, with which no general principles will furnish us. In consequence of this, the detail, the reality, has to be supplied by the Utopian romancer, from states of society already realised in the past or the present. The new principles are then superimposed upon a basis already formed of old principles, and a hybrid pseudo-reality is produced, which is neither past, present, nor future. When we ourselves are part and parcel of a social state, when we ourselves are a portion of the reality of a given society, bathed in its categories and inhaling its atmosphere, our imagination cannot transcend it to any appreciable extent, if at all. Our logical faculty can, indeed, as it were, dissolve the present social reality for abstract thought, and show the lines on which the new principle growing up within it is going, but our imagination is quite incapable of envisaging the future social reality in its completed shape. We can just as little conceive how the men of the future will envisage our civilisation of to-day – how they will represent to themselves our thoughts and feelings, aspirations and antipathies – for when all this social life has become objective, with its categories stiff and lifeless, it will be seen in its true proportions and significance. To illustrate the truth of the foregoing, we have only to recall the impossibility the modern man finds in freeing himself from the illusion of Pessimism, the outcome of which is the Cynicism proper to the superior person of century-end "culture." Our intellectual insight, which tells us that this, too, must pass, as surely as the pessimism of the decaying classical world passed, or as the optimism of the eighteenth century has passed, that it is a mere mood bred of a mephitic social atmosphere, generated in its turn by the rank overgrowth of an effete civilisation – this intellectual insight may, I say, preserve us from the priggish and ostentatious cynicism of the superior person, but it does not free us from the oppression now and again of the feeling (embodied in all modern literature and art) that the world has grown old – that for humanity, das Lied ist aus. This feeling we can just as little rid ourselves of, because we know it has no basis, except in ourselves, than we can rid ourselves of the optical illusion that the sun is moving, because we know that the earth, and not the sun, moves.

The author hopes, in conclusion, that the present volume may stimulate the thought of some in certain directions, as he has reason to believe its predecessors have, in some slight degree, been instrumental in doing.

E.B.B.

I

1. The Orator of the Human Race

From Outlooks from the New Standpoint, pp.1-37.

The eighteenth century was in full swing. Louis Quinze furniture decorated the houses of the wealthy. "Wit," "verses," and carefully elaborated repartee varied by excursions into the regions of "philosophy," formed the staple of social intercourse in the salons of the aforesaid houses. Travelling was not much no easy or less attended with danger than had been the case in the previous century. "Crackskull Heath" and distinguished highwaymen in the environs of London were living realities. The superstructure of feudal Europe – withered and dead – was still standing in its main outlines. The new culture of the "age of reason" had not as yet penetrated to any considerable extent below the surface of society, that is the wealthy and educated classes, although signs were not wanting of its beginning to do so. Such was the world – the world of Goethe's Dichtung und Wahrheit, and the world of Rousseau's Confessions – into which the future Orator of the Human Race was born.

Jean-Baptiste Cloots, or Klootz, first saw the light on the 24th of June 1755 in the valley of Gnadenthal, a few miles from the town of Cleves, near the Dutch frontier of Westphalia. His father, the Baron Von Cloots, possessed a chateau in the midst of a well-cultivated domain. The Cloots family, though an ancient line of nobility, had acquired wealth in the then leading commercial city of Amsterdam, sometime during the seventeenth century. The district of Cleves, during the infancy of Jean-

Baptiste, was the scene of many a squabble between Frederick the Great and the French king. Frederick would throw off a satirical rhyme on the poetical effusions of a cardinal who happened to be the favourite of one of the many royal mistresses of France. The peasants of Cleves were made the scapegoats. The valley was pillaged and the inhabitants butchered to make a Franco-Prussian holiday. Incidents such as this occurred more than once during the childhood of Cloots. The old baron thought fit on such occasions to prudently make friends with the mammon of unrighteousness as exemplified in the invaders, by inviting the officers to his chateau and handsomely entertaining them. In this way little Jean-Baptiste became early acquainted with the French language, French manners, and French modes of thought. His one desire, on the departure of the French soldiery, was to be educated in Paris with a view to a career in the French court. His father not being unwilling that he should make his name in the leading society of Europe, consented, and before long he found himself in the city of his dreams, the city of that Voltaire of whom he had so often heard from his French friends, and with whose renown at that time all Europe rang. The clerical education he received at the Sorbonne produced a strong reaction in him. He took to eating omelettes au lard on Friday and audaciously inviting his school-fellows to join him. At the table of the Dutch banker, Vandenhyver, through whom his allowance was paid, he heard of the philosophers so execrated at the Sorbonne; how their writings had been burnt and how they themselves existed, so to speak, only on sufferance, since by virtue of an old edict they might be hanged any day. Here also he learnt for the first time that his uncle, Cornelius de Pauw, although a canon, was himself a philosopher, but so far from being in danger of the rope, was a leading light at the court of the King of Prussia – the friend and protector of Voltaire himself. Jean-Baptiste, finding out that the leader of eighteenth century literature did not habitually live in Paris as he had thought, immediately conceived the idea of hurrying off to Berlin to make friends with his free-thinking relative. He left Paris and repaired to his native valley, where he was greeted with enthusiasm by his father, who now saw in his rapid physical development the earnest of a future officer in the land of Grenadiers. What could be a nobler avocation than to serve a philosophic king, the friend and protector of philosophers? thought our hero at this time. So Jean-Baptiste readily consented to his father's wishes that he should enter the military school of Berlin. He had not been long there, however, before he discovered in common with his instructors that soldiering was not his vocation, though he did not definitively give up his intention of joining the army for some years.

His sojourn in the capital of Brandenburg was otherwise not unimportant for the future Orator. The court was in the neighbouring town of Potsdam. He there spoke face to face with the great Frederick and with the great Frederick's friend, his uncle Cornelius, from the latter of whom he received his first distinctive intellectual bent. Cured of certain intellectual vanities in which he had nursed himself, he began to study seriously, and at last disgusted with the slavery and brutality of the Prussian military régime, he sought and obtained the king's permission to return home – his ultimate intention being to take up his abode once more in Paris. He was now twenty-one years of age, and the possessor of an income of 100,000 livres. It was some six or seven years since he had left the city which was the capital of eighteenth-century culture, and everything now appeared to him in a new light. He entered the Parisian salons and mixed freely in society; he came into contact with Benjamin Franklin, then on a political mission to Paris. But Jean-Baptiste was not destined to see his idol, Voltaire, for the latter expired a few days after his arrival in Paris at the Hotel de Villette. An idea already conceived while in Berlin now began to take definite shape in Cloots's mind – that, namely, of developing a refutation of all revealed religions from one proposition, or rather, syllogism. With this syllogism which he used to call "his Great Argument," he was fond of dumbfounding his clerical acquaintances. It ran as follows:

1.A religion of which the proofs are not comprehensible by all reasonable men cannot be established by God for the simple and ignorant.

2.Now, there is no religion of all those which are pretended to have been revealed of which the proofs are comprehensible by all men. Therefore:

3.None of the religions which pretend to be revealed can be the religion established by God for the simple and ignorant.

The determination to work out this argument in book-form took increasing possession of Jean-Baptiste, till he resolved to retire for some months to Gnadenthal for the purpose of putting his project into execution; as a matter of fact, he remained there more than a year laboriously working at his Certitude of the Proofs of Mahometism, designed as a reductio ad absurdam of supernaturalism. The book was published in Amsterdam. As soon as it issued from the press, Cloots despatched the whole edition to Paris, at the same time hurrying thither himself. To his intense surprise, the "Great Argument" and the Certitude of the Proofs of Mahometism alike fell dead. By no device could the author succeed in obtaining even a partial success. Undeterred, Cloots tried debating societies, but here the clerical opposition was too strong for him. At last one of the leading Paris clergy delivered a pulpit oration against Certitudes, by which it achieved some little notoriety, though far short of the expectations of its enthusiastic author.

Cloots now began to occupy himself with the second great principle to which he proposed to devote his life. Up to this time he had been too much engaged with the notion of establishing

13

reason on the ruins of the ancient faith to think of anything else. The international problem now began to occupy him. In the Views of a Gallophile, he offered to the world his first distinct statement of the doctrine of Internationalism. As yet, however, his opinions had not attained the breadth or definiteness of those expounded in his later work, the Universal Republic. Seized with a desire to study English institutions, which he had heard so much be-praised in the salons of Paris, Cloots crossed the channel, came to London, was disgusted with the dingy, brick-built houses he saw, which he compared unfavourably with the masonry of Paris; visited Edmund Burke at Beaconsfield, discussed with him the new ideas and dawning hopes, and tried to imbue him with his own enthusiasm for everything French. Burke, who had not as yet become insane and reactionary, proved a sympathetic auditor, for although old enough to be his guest's father, he still retained much of his youthful freshness. The two men got on excellently together, and Cloots left London with a pressing invitation from the English statesman to pay him another visit. He returned to Paris, but at the beginning of the winter left for the house of a relative near Amsterdam. While in Holland he had a narrow escape of being victimised by a charlatan from the east of Europe, who gave himself out for a descendant of Scanderbeg, and as the Prince of Roumania. However, Cloots came out of the adventure with nothing more serious than a temporary loss of dignity. In the spring, resisting the attraction which Paris once more had for him, Jean-Baptiste resolved to enjoy the freedom, instruction, and adventures of a long tour throughout the greater part of Europe. This journey, however, proved more often of the nature of a flight than of a tour. Taking no care to conceal his views on such delicate subjects as the prerogative of kings and nobles and the value of a sacerdotal class, not unfrequently preaching open rebellion to oppressed peasants, we may imagine his path was not always strewn with roses. He was being once nearly arrested on Prussian territory, while he had to fly from Hungary for protesting against the tyrannous acts of the king and emperor. In Italy he fared no better. The beginning of the winter found him in the south of France, at Bayonne. From thence he proceeded to Spain, and from thence to Morocco, where the author of the ironical Certitude of the Proofs of Mahometism was, it appears, well received alike by the Moorish and Jewish population, he having championed the Hebrew race against the Christians in a pamphlet on the Jewish question. After a stay of a few weeks he proceeded to Lisbon, where he remained for the rest of the winter. New Year's Day, 1789, found Cloots enjoying the mild sea breezes and blue sky of Portugal, and looking over the Atlantic with thoughts tending to America as the only country of the "Rights of Man." During the winter Cloots continued for the most part cut off from news of the outer world, but with the approach of spring came the tidings of the rehabilitation of the popular idol Neckar, and of the convocation of the "States-General," with a double representation of the third estate. Cloots left Lisbon with the intention of proceeding by easy stages to Paris. Some weeks elapsed, however, before he crossed the Pyrennees.

He had scarcely set foot on French soil when the report reached him of the fall of the Bastille. With all the enthusiasm of his character he donned the new tri-coloured cockade, and proceeded in hot haste to the city which was henceforth to be for him the metropolis of the "Human Race." He passed through a country which presented, in some respects, the aspect of an invaded territory. The sight of burning, or recently burnt, châteaus – of crops destroyed – of houses pillaged – was quite a common one. Arrived in Paris, Cloots immediately threw himself into the thick of the political struggle. His social connexions brought him into close contact with several of the leaders of the "States-General," now converted into the "National Constituent Assembly." This was to our hero the germ of that parliament of man, of which he had long dreamed, and which at last took definite shape in his mind as the goal of his political aspirations. At this time Cloots might have been daily seen riding about Paris from centre to centre in his carriage and pair, accompanied by two servants, themselves ardent patriots, in order to ascertain the true political temperature of the capital. After some days he decided upon a propagandist journey into what was supposed to be the most benighted province of France – Brittany. He found there what are described as: "Certain fierce animals, male and female, scattered about the country, black, living, but quite burnt by the sun, attached to the earth which they hoed and dug with invincible obstinacy." To Jean-Baptiste, nevertheless, these degraded creatures were brothers. By means of an interpreter he overcame the obstacle of the Breton language, and for days and weeks he went about the country preaching to them the doctrine of the "Rights of Man" and of the Revolution. At first, ill-understood, they gave him ear when he explained to them the two recent decrees of the Assembly, abolishing the local imposts and practically establishing the right of peasant proprietory. Finally the peasants were seized as if by inspiration with the spirit of revolt. Emulating the Parisians, they stormed, torch in hand, the château of their lord, the local Bastille. The movement rapidly spread, and soon wherever Jean-Baptiste had passed, the cry was unanimous of – "Long live the Revolution of the National Assembly."

After establishing a Breton Club, Cloots returned to Paris in October to find the Assembly and the king installed in the capital, consequent on the events of the 5th and 6th of the month. When Cloots caught sight once more of the towers of Notre Dame, he vowed never again to leave the world-city, and he never did. His motto – "Paris! France! Universe!" was henceforth to be defended from the centre itself. Famine still reigned in Paris. Yet, notwithstanding the terrible misery, what was Cloots' astonishment and delight to find that even in St. Antoine, he heard more among the groups of workmen assembled, about the "Rights of Man," and the "Principles of the Constitution," than about bread! Cloots now became an assiduous attendant at the

Palais Royal, which was the great open-air resort of patriots and the forum for popular discussion. Not far off in the Rue St. Honoré was the Jacobins Club. The district was nick-named the "Quartier de l'Idée." Reports of royal conspiracies filled the air. Nobles who had remained in Paris were breathing out threatening and slaughter against the Revolution. Jean-Baptiste soon found their society insupportable; the only answer he got to his pleadings on behalf of the people was: "Let the people perish, we want our pensions." Cloots shook the dust of these noble houses off his feet and cursed them bitterly. His place was henceforth in the Faubourg, in popular gatherings, in the public tribunes of the Assembly. Meanwhile Burke had denounced the French Revolution in the English parliament. Cloots we may be sure was not long in publishing an open letter to his friend full of affectionate remonstrance and entreaty. He was awaiting a reply to this missive, when all thought of Burke was forgotten in the news that the Assembly had assigned to the nation the right of making peace or war. Cloots was seized with a wild enthusiasm – he saw in this the beginning of the realisation of the solidarity of the Human Race. Was it not kings and nobles who had hitherto set people against people? Once the power of declaring war was removed from their hands, would not the chief cause of war have disappeared? The re-arrangement of the map of France by which the semi-autonomy of the old French provinces had been abolished, all tended towards the unity of mankind, he thought. From all sides was the cry – "We are no longer Provencals, Bretons, Angeves, Picards – we are Frenchmen!" Cloots saw in this also a step toward the federation of the Human Race, rather than, as was actually the case, the embodiment of the modern principle of nationalism as against the local autonomy of the middle-ages.

On the 5th of June, 1790, the Paris municipality, after proclaiming all men brothers, proposed that the Assembly should decree a great fête for the ensuing 14th of July, the anniversary of the fall of the Bastille, which should embrace representatives from all France. Jean-Baptiste was transported beyond measure. We will have, said he, "not merely a festival of France but of the Universe." He forthwith proceeded to hunt up all the foreign refugees in Paris he could lay his hand on. At his instigation they formed themselves into a committee, with the result that, on the 19th of the month, they appeared at the bar of the Assembly praying for admission to the National Federation. The deputation was a remarkable one, thirty-six members in all; each wore his national costume; Neopolitan, Spaniard, Prussian, Dutchman, Englishman, American, all had a place, while an Arab and a Chaldean were to be seen on either side of the deputed Orator. Cloots began (silence having been proclaimed by the usher):

"Gentlemen, the imposing group of all the banners of the French Empire will be displayed on the 14th of July in the Champ de Mars, on the same spot where Julian trampled down all prejudices, and where Charlemagne surrounded himself with all the virtues. This civic solemnity will not only be the festival of the French, but also be the festival of the Human Race. The trumpet which sounded the resurrection of the great people, has reached to all the four quarters of the world, and the songs of rejoicing of twenty-five million free men have awakened nations buried in a long slavery. The wisdom of your decrees, gentlemen, is the union of the children of France. This ravishing picture affords bitter apprehensions to despots, and just hopes to enslaved peoples ... You have truly recognised that sovereignty resides in the people. Now the people is everywhere under the yoke of dictators, who call themselves sovereigns in defiance of your principles. They usurp the dictatorship, but the sovereignty is inviolable, and the ambassadors of these tyrants would not be able to honour your august festival like ourselves, of whom, for the most part, the mission is tacitly avowed by our compatriots, the oppressed sovereigns themselves."

18

The applause, which at several times interrupted Jean-Baptiste while speaking, fairly shook the house when he had ended. The reply of the Assembly, from the lips of its chairman, the Baron Menou, was an invitation couched in terms overflowing with compliments and cordiality. The Arab returned thanks in an unintelligible French, and the ceremony was wound up with some dexterous phrases of the president. In its transport of enthusiasm the Assembly then passed its memorable decree abolishing the titles and insignia of nobility. Henceforth Jean-Baptiste rejoiced in bearing the proud title of the "Orator of the Human Race." But the enthusiasm of this memorable night was short-lived, and began to give place to ridicule within a few days, a result which was not diminished by the discovery that the interesting figures of the Turk and the Arab had been borrowed from the opera, and that the would-be Chaldean had been born within sight of the towers of Notre Dame.

At last the long looked-for day of the national fête arrived. To the great disappointment of all it poured with rain. "God is an aristocrat," said some of the crowd. "I could have told you that long ago," said Jean-Baptiste; but the weather made little difference to our hero, who marched to the Champ de Mars at the head of his international cortege in a state of moral exaltation, which rendered physical discomfort of no account. His description of the fête, in a letter to female friend, Fanny de Beauharnais, testifies to the spirit in which he viewed the ceremony of the day, which must have been, in truth, imposing enough. "It transports you," he writes, "two thousand years back, by I know not what colour of antiquity. It transports you two thousand years forward by that rapid progress of reason, of which this federation is the delectable foretaste." This state of moral intoxication seems to have lasted for several days. He now bethought himself of his Christian pre-nomen. How could he, the apostle of reason and the enemy of all supernatural cults, continue to bear a name derived from the creed which had enslaved the Human Race for so many centuries past? He must seek a name more befitted to his position, derived from some ancient hero or thinker. Turning this over in his mind, he hit upon the cognomen, Anacharsis that of the Scythian disciple of Greek culture, who had been popularised by the recently published romance of the Abbé Barthelemy. It was the very thing as it seemed to him, for he too was a barbarian who had expatriated himself in the modern Athens, and had embraced its modes of thought and manners of life. Jean-Baptiste Cloots, Baron of Gnadenthal, vassal of the King of Prussia, shall be known from this time forward under the style and title of "Anacharsis Cloots, Orator of the Human Race, Representative of the Oppressed Sovereign Peoples of Mankind."

Cloots now began to jealously watch the actions of the powers, and the developments of French foreign policy, fearing lest France should be led into a trap, but he did not neglect his propaganda in Paris, in connexion with his anti-religious crusade. He became a member of the Jacobins Club, and also of a society which met in the circus of the Palais Royal and called itself the Cercle Social des Amis de la Vérité, a leading figure in which was the mystical revolutionary priest and afterwards bishop, Claude Fauchet, with whom the atheist Anacharsis had many a passage of arms. He also busied himself with addresses, pamphlets, and newspaper articles, writing constantly in the Chronique de Paris, founded by his friend Charles Villette, and edited by another acquaintance named Millin – for notwithstanding his democratic attitude he was still a welcome guest amongst the "advanced" circles of the wealthy classes. Among the letters of adhesion to his principles were some from notable foreigners. The Countess of Hesse among others wrote proclaiming herself a convert to his views. In this life of social and literary activity he passed the year 1791. After the flight of the king to Varennes, Anacharsis was the first to demand the abolition of the monarchy and to proclaim the French Republic as

20

the necessary first step to that Universal Republic which was the goal of his political action. He was one of the leaders in the July meeting in the Champ de Mars with the members of the Cordeliers Club, etc.; though after the massacre of Lafayette, on the evening of that day, and the decree proclaiming martial law which followed it, Cloots, in common with the other men of the advanced party, was compelled to "lie low" for a while. Brissot with his Girondin friends was already beginning his campaign against Paris in the pretended interest of the departments.

With the spring of 1792 the political horizon began to show storm-clouds. The debates in the Jacobins became noisier and more acrimonious. The great question of the war raised its head, and with it previous differences between Cloots and the Girondin leaders, notably Brissot, as also at times with Robespierre, began to accentuate themselves. Cloots was in favour of a propagandist war on a large scale; Brissot of a defensive war; and Robespierre of no war at all. Anacharsis thought by an offensive war to liberate once for all the neighbouring "Sovereigns" (bien entendu sovereign peoples) from the yoke of their tyrants, and therewith to inaugurate the era of Universal Peace. Brissot's one thought was a defensive war, which should protect the frontiers and remove the centre of revolutionary interest from Paris to the departments; while Robespierre, though desirous of maintaining the ascendancy of Paris, was even more averse than Brissot to the cosmopolitan theories of Cloots. With the declaration of war and the first reverses of the French troops the excitement in Paris became so intense that internal dissensions among the "patriots" were for the nonce laid on one side. The ascendancy of Paris seemed secured for the time being at least. It was at this juncture that Cloots published his famous brochure, the "Universal Republic," in which he expounded his views as to mankind constituting one nation whose metropolis should be Paris.

"The crowd," says he, "attracts the crowd, and deserts repel men. It is essential for the universal harmony to have a common capital where all divergent lights unite in a focus; where all characters adjust each other; where all prejudices are abolished; where all egotism are crushed and confounded in the common interest of the Human Race. It is here that the man of the Department becomes the man of France, that the man of France becomes the man of the Universe."

At last Brunswick, passing the Rhine, launched his celebrated manifesto threatening to annihilate the Revolution. The whole revolutionary city now took up as with one voice the cry of "déchèance," which had been on the lips of Anacharsis for more than a year past. The movement of the 10th of August began to prepare. Cloots agitated amongst the Dutch and Belgium refugees, who formed the nucleus of the foreign legion known as the Légion Franche. The word Sans-Culotte at this time became the vogue to designate the popular party of Paris. Anacharsis proclaimed himself the Orator of the Sans-Culottes. In vain did his mother the baroness (the old baron had been dead for some time) write urging him to fly from the dangers which surrounded him. He only replied in a long letter explaining the principles of the Revolution, and declaring his adhesion to them come what might, at the same time assuring her that serious disorder would never occur in Paris. "I shall never quit France," he said, "and they shall never take Paris except the conquerors are invulnerable." He urges her not to believe the lies circulated respecting the Revolution and its adherents. "Adieu, my tender mother," he concludes, "your health disquiets me more than our enemies."

In the early morning of the memorable 10th of August Cloots awoke to the sound of the tocsin and the alarm drum, and hurriedly rising rushed to the Assembly, while two of his servants

22

made for the Tuilleries. Anacharsis remained for two days and nights among the legislators. He saw the king himself appear in the Salle de Mainège; he heard the decree for the summoning of a National Convention; he was the instrument in arresting a princely spy in the court-yard. The next night he appeared at the bar of the Assembly with some compatriots offering to form a Prussian legion. The Assembly ordered the printing and distribution in the departments of the address he delivered on this occasion. On the 24th a decree was passed for the naturalisation, with the full rights as French citizens, of certain eminent foreigners, amongst whom Cloots was included side by side with Thomas Paine, Priestly, etc. The only member who spoke in opposition to this, Thuriot, was immediately voted down. Cloots as French citizen was now eligible for election for the Convention, and he was nominated amid general approbation candidate for the department of the Oise, where he had recently bought a small property adjoining that of his friend Charles Villette, and also for the department of the Saone-et-Loire.

At the end of the month the news arrived that Longwy had been taken by the Prussians and that Verdun was threatened. This meant, as all knew well enough, that Paris itself was in imminent danger. The consequence was the September massacres, that terrible act of justice and self-defence of revolutionary France towards the traitors on her hearth. Anacharsis was assiduous in his attendance at the primary assembly of his section during this time, although he had no share in organising the work that was being done. It was on the 3rd of September, and on behalf of his section, that Anacharsis visited the Rolands, where he remained to dinner at the special invitation of the Minister of the Interior, in company with the principal lights of the Girondist party – a dinner alluded to in the celebrated "Memoirs" in a tone of more than questionable taste, as regards the subject of the present sketch. Marat, with the ready suspicion characteristic of his noble but narrow nature, had just been denouncing our Orator for the second time as a Mouchard Berlinois, when the same evening Cloots presented himself at the Jacobins Club. He was being considerably hustled and was like to be driven out of the club, when the intimation arrived of his election for the département de l'Oise. At this announcement the hustling and jeering ceased, but the Girondin and other Moderates were not slow to take advantage of it in trying to prejudice Cloots against Paris, which had rejected him, and in favour of the departments which had accepted him, for his election for the Saone-et-Loire was shortly after announced also. But the Orator was too sincere to be influenced by mere personal considerations, and in spite of all temptations he remained true to Paris.

The battle between the Parisian Sans-Culottes, represented in the Convention by the so-called party of the Mountain and the departmental Girondins, now began in real earnest. All Cloots's social connexions naturally brought him into contact with the anti-Parisian party, who were in power. The "Orator of the Human Race" was, indeed, made president of the Diplomatic Committee, one of the twenty-four Committees into which the Convention had resolved itself, and though he was powerless as regards the positive furtherance of his own principles of foreign policy on this Committee, yet it enabled him to expose the intrigues of the dominant Moderates with doubtful generals, and with the enemy, in the hope of patching-up a peace in order to have their hands free to crush Paris. Singularly enough, the event which caused him to take a decisive position on the summit of the "Mountain" was the Girondist attack headed by Louvet, on his subsequent persecutor and murderer, Robespierre. The accusations levelled against the latter were understood by all as in reality levelled against the entire Mountain and against Paris. Anacharsis was surrounded by Mountainist deputies, to whom forgetting the speaker in the tribune, he narrated the whole history of anti-Parisian chicanery. Urged by the Mountain to publish what he had told them, he

24

hesitated to reveal the official secrets of his Committee, until the open treachery of Dumouriez and others and the discovery of actually treasonable correspondence, decided him to throw away all scruples and expose the whole proceedings of the Committee men. He now published his pamphlet, Ni Marat, Ni Roland, in which he attacked the principle of leadership. This pamphlet was greeted with applause by all patriots, not excepting Marat himself, and the Jacobins ordered its distribution in the departments.

The Orator a few days after launched an address to the Belgians denouncing the federalism of Roland and his associates, persuading them to constitute the newly-acquired province into a second republic. He still further exposed governmental intrigues, and concluded: "Brave Belgians, choose deliberately between Departmental unity, which combines the maximum of independence with the maximum of economy, and Republican plurality, which unites the maximum of expense with the maximum of absurdity" The Convention now appointed a commission to investigate the incriminatory documents discovered in the baggage left by the officers who had fled across the frontier. To the consternation of Roland and his clique, Anacharsis formed one of the Committee. On the occasion when this proposition was voted, he had the satisfaction of making friends with Marat, who apologised for having called him a mouchard under a false impression, and embraced him as a "bon enfant." Cloots a few nights afterwards justified himself at the Jacobins against the ministerial attack. He was surrounded by all the members of the Mountain, who declared he had saved the country. It was at no little cost to himself, however, that Cloots had taken up his position definitely as a Sans-Culotte and Mountainist. The doors of the wealthy houses he used to visit at, and where he had many friends to whom he was personally attached, were henceforth closed to him. He had to break with almost all the sct who had before regarded him as an amiable

25

crank. The journals in which he used to write now became impossible for him. The Girondists and Moderates were his bitterest enemies, but he had the proud feeling that he helped to save the unity of France and the "idea of the propaganda." He began to occupy himself with organising the foreign Legion and drawing up further addresses to the Dutch and Belgians. On the occasion of the king's trial he voted on each issue with the majority. Active work in the Convention on behalf of Paris and the Mountain against the Girondists; pamphlets, addresses, journalism, especially the new Franco-Dutch organ Le Batave occupied his time for the next few weeks. The conflict waxed hotter. The gauntlet was thrown to the Girondists by the Jacobins when the latter elected Marat as their president. Next followed the abortive prosecution of Marat and his triumphal acquittal.

At the beginning of May, Cloots was prostrated by a severe gastric attack accompanied by fever, doubtless brought on, in part, at least, by the strain of excitement and overwork in which he was living. For nearly a month he was confined to his bed in a more or less unconscious or delirious state. He recovered to find the Revolution of the second of June, 1793, an accomplished fact. Surely his dreams were now about to be realised! Paris had triumphed, and, in spite of the treachery of generals and ministers, the boundaries of the great French Republic would yet be extended to the Scheldt and the Rhine. The reorganised Paris Commune with Hébert and Chaumette at its head, and with Pache as mayor, was in many ways the principal public body in France. But the Convention had appointed two Committees, a Committee of Public Safety, to whom the ministers were responsible, and a larger Committee of General Security. These Committees were the power to which the Convention delegated the executive authority. They were at first provisional, but their powers were afterwards prolonged and increased. Robespierre, the old Constitutionalist and now Mountainist Barère, St. Just, and Carnot were amongst the members of the former Committee. Robespierre now began to show himself in his true colours, and he soon became the leading spirit in the executive. His vanity, priggishness, and lack of all ideal led him to give ear to the blandishments of a certain Soulavie, who, at that time, represented the French Republic at Geneva. This personage, who was an ex-Jesuit, persuaded Robespierre that it was necessary for the conclusion of peace that France should immediately show her intention of abandoning all thought, once for all, of an aggressive war; should restrain her frontiers within the old limits; and, finally, should keep the revolutionary spirit within such bounds as would render it acceptable to the reactionary powers. This view was adopted by Barère, and acquiesced in by the other members of the Committee of Public Safety. Hence, in spite of divergence of view as regards internal political organisation, the party of Robespierre was just as anxious for a patched-up peace on the basis of subservience to the foreign coalition as the now proscribed and imprisoned Girondists had been. Meanwhile, affairs on the frontiers became desperate. Mainz had been surrendered to the Prussians; Valenciennes and Condé had fallen into the hands of the English and Austrians; the road to Paris was once more open to Brunswick; in short, the military situation at the end of August, 1793, appeared if anything still more desperate than it had been the same time the previous year. Result: the terror once more "the order of the day," this time however, so far as Paris was concerned, not taking the form of massacres, but of a suddenly increased activity of the guillotine. Suspicion and the wildest of alarmist reports were matters of course; hope, fear, desperation, alternating and mingling in the vortex of political excitement made men tigers like Carrier, or crazed fanatics like Lebon. But amid all the horrors of the time, and the temporary eclipse of the dawning hopes of a sudden and indefinite extension of the frontiers of Sans-Culottism, there was one bright streak rapidly widening on the horizon which compensated for everything else in the eyes of the "Orator of the Human Race" – and this was the growing renunciation by all classes of the

27

Christian faith and the open adoption of Reason as the basis of belief. Cloots, now installed by the Mountain as member of the Committee of Education, was daily busy in formulating a scheme of instruction according to the principles of Reason and the Revolution. He felt this no less important than his speeches and action in the Convention itself. But the most striking event in which Anacharsis at this time took part was the inauguration of the worship of Reason, in which, in conjunction with the Hébertist party, he was the leading spirit. From September onwards, the number of clerical resignations and of renunciations by public bodies of Catholicism augmented daily. At last the Commune agreed to demand the institution of a great public fête to celebrate the installation of Reason and freedom of conscience, in the place occupied by God and the Church. The twentieth of the newly instituted month, Brumaire, was selected as the day of celebration. The movement received a further edge from the news arriving that the Vendéan insurgents had re-united with the Bretons, and in the name of King and Church had crossed the Loire with the intention of marching on to Paris. The very same evening at eleven o'clock, Anacharsis, fresh from a crowded meeting of the Jacobins, in which the abolition of the "cult" had been enthusiastically resolved upon, accompanied by two other deputies, proceeded to the residence of Gobel, the Archbishop of Paris, to demand his abjuration of the Christian faith, or, at least, of his public functions. Gobel knew that the Commune had decreed the seizure of Church property, and that in accordance with this decree large quantities of Church plate had already been sent in for public purposes; so, after a moment's hesitation, he agreed, having first stipulated that he should summon his chapter. Cloots and his friends next proceeded to the Pantheon, the ci-devant Church of St. Genevieve, for the purpose of destroying the statue of the saint. Next morning they again visited the archbishop. This time he received them surrounded by his chapter, who by fourteen votes to three had decided in favour of abdication and of joining the fête. Anacharsis hurried off to the Commune to inform Chaumette of the good news. The latter did

28

not know the Orator personally, although he esteemed his views. The two men embraced each other for the first time, and the son of the vine-dresser and of the privy counsellor of the King of Prussia – Anaxagoras Chaumette, and Anacharsis Cloots – went arm in arm to the council of the department, where the councillors departmental and municipal were to muster for the procession to the Convention. Gobel and his chapter they found already en route. Arrived at the Convention, a strange scene presented itself. The archbishop and his chapter, bonnetrouge on head, were at the bar of the Convention formally laying down their insignia of office – cross, ring, mitre, and Gothic box – Gobel renouncing in a few words the functions of the Catholic cultus. Other clergy followed in the same strain. Chaumette demanded that the Committee of public instruction should appoint a day in the recently instituted calender to be dedicated to Reason. The president then announced the establishment of the new religion: "The Supreme Being only requires the practice of social and moral virtues: such is his religion. He desires no cult but that of Reason. This shall be henceforth the National Religion." He then embraced the ex-archbishop. A crowd more clergy followed declaring their renunciation of the old faith, and in many cases also of the pensions attached to their functions. The hall was brought down by tumultuous applause from the popular tribunes. Cloots and his friends of the Commune were in ecstasies. The former hurried off to proclaim the joyful news to the Committee of Public Safety. He burst in upon Robespierre and his colleagues at the Pavilion Flore with a torrent of enthusiasm, describing the events that had taken place. To his intense astonishment he was greeted with a marked coolness. Robespierre even ventured to take him to task for alienating the Belgians by the insult to the Catholic faith. A brief altercation ensued which ended in the "Incorruptible" turning his back upon our Orator, muttering at the same time the word "masquerades." The cold-blooded traitor was already contemplating the destruction of the advanced section of the Revolutionary party, whose consistency and idealism stood in the way of his own ambitious plans. How could he become the head of a regenerated middle-class France, so long as foreign enthusiasts were preaching the extension of frontier in the interests of the Republic of the Human Race, and fanatics, native and foreign alike, were disestablishing the Church in the interests of an atheistic cultus? Cloots was depressed on leaving the Committee, but the enthusiasm he everywhere encountered soon raised his spirits again. The new movement for the time being carried all before it. The extension of the frontier to the Rhine and the universal establishment of the new religion were for the nonce the rallying-cry all round. The coolness and veiled opposition of the Robespierre-party became a subject of general comment. The Commune, indeed, declared the Committee of Public Safety to have become a public danger, inasmuch as it refused to keep pace with the Revolution. In the midst of the apparent triumph of Sans-Culottism, the cloud no bigger than a man's hand, destined to destroy it, was already spreading. The great fête of the twentieth of Brumaire, however, was not only held as all the world knows in Paris, but was the inauguration of similar fêtes throughout the length and breadth of Revolutionary France during the ensuing weeks. The allegorical figure of the goddess of reason, which has so often been ridiculed, was really a piece of symbolism fully in accordance with the imitative classicism of eighteenth century thought. The idea, when properly carried out, must have been the occasion of a pleasant pageant.

As soon as the first excitement had died down a little, Robespierre and the Committee-men began taking their measures. The immediate aim of the "Incorruptible" was to win over the Jacobins Club in which he had a considerable number or partizans. The Cordeliers Club was hopelessly on the side of the Sans-Culottists, and henceforward became their chief stronghold. But Anacharsis was just now at the height of his influence. In spite of Robespierre and his friends he had been elected to the presidency of the Jacobins. In this capacity, on the reception of

Chalier, the president of the Lyons branch of the Club, he proclaimed: "One day all patriots will unite for the maintenance of the Universal Republic, and the welfare of their brothers! What do I say? They will all be brothers, and the Universe will be but one temple, having the firmament for its dome!" But while the "Orator of the Human Race" was expounding these doctrines in the Rue St. Honoré, Robespierre was unfolding his scheme of foreign policy at the Tuilleries, speciously promising peace and a return of prosperity as a reward for what was tantamount to handing over to him complete control of the reins of power. Outside the Convention hall he was supported by the bulk of the middle classes, especially the shopkeepers, who dreaded the "excesses" of the popular party, and who found their businesses at a standstill.

It was getting patent indeed to everyone that the idealistic views and aspirations of Cloots and the Hébertist party, which were shared in by the bulk of the working-class population of Paris and the large towns, were inconsistent with the "respectable" subservient policy which the Committee led by Robespierre was bent on pursuing. The Committee began, tentatively at first, to follow out the plan of immolating its antagonists by the arrest of two questionable deputies, Chabot and Basire. The Committee-men were supported in the Convention and the press by what constituted now the extreme wing of the moderate party, the Dantonists. The destruction of Cloots was the next thing determined on by the "Incorruptible" as an urgent act of grace towards the powers, especially Prussia, which was supposed to be more favourable to France than Austria. Reports were industriously circulated as to Cloots being a foreign agent, whose design was to ruin France by inducing her to enter upon impracticable schemes of foreign conquest which would lay her territories open to invasion; and also through apparent zeal for the Revolution to discredit it by excesses.

The first thing to do was to get him out of the Jacobins Club. Accordingly Robespierre obtained a resolution for its purification from members who, on investigation, might prove undesirable. On the evening of the sitting, when the obnoxious members were to be challenged, two hours before the time of opening, the doors were besieged by an excited crowd. As much as twenty livres were offered for a seat. The spacious hall in the Rue St. Honoré was thronged with Philosophers, Jacobins, Federalists, and Dantonists. Cloots was there betimes surrounded by Mountainist deputies and partizans of the Commune. "Purification" commenced; several members having been challenged, some passing the ordeal, others being excluded, it came to the turn of Robespierre. He ascended the tribune, but (bad augury for Cloots) was allowed to descend again amid a storm of applause without even being interrogated. At last Cloots was called upon. The usual questions as to name, birthplace, occupation, etc., having been answered amid a breathless silence, a Robespierreist voice from the middle of the hall was heard to croak: "I like Anacharsis much, I esteem his public spirit, but I could wish to have some explanation as to his relations with Vandenhyver." Vandenhyver was the banker through whom Cloots had received his allowance during his student years, and who had been recently guillotined on the ground of Royalist intrigue with Du-Barry. Cloots quickly and conclusively showed what his relations with Vandeallyver had been. He had just concluded when the great "Incorruptible" himself rose to his feet, and in a poisonous harangue carefully adapted to stimulate the suspicions and prejudices of an excited Paris audience, he denounced his victim as a Prussian baron who had been in the habit of visiting the counter-revolutionary enemies of France. He next proceeded to attack the movement against the "cult" of which he sought to show Cloots to have been the mainspring. This movement, he declared, tended by its violence to jeopardise the entire Revolution. The interview of Cloots with the Committee on the day of the abdication of Gobel was then brought up against him. In lachrymose tones the arch hypocrite

32

talked about his mission and that of the Committee being finished if such traitors as Cloots were permitted to work in their midst. "Cloots," he wound up, "is a Prussian; I have traced the history of his political life for you. Pronounce!" The Orator was dumfounded at this succession of foul blows. Immense excitement reigned throughout the hall. Cloots was about to rise in reply, when from the middle of the audience a proposition was made for which urgency was demanded – a proposition to exclude from the society bankers, foreigners, nobles, to which were added by a piece of clever trickery designed to throw dust in the eyes of the Sans-Culottes – priests. The motion was hurriedly put and carried. Anacharsis found himself expelled from the society without having had the chance of saying a word in his own defence. The affair had been arranged with a fiendish ingenuity by one of the greatest masters in political roguery the world has ever seen.

Cloots, although staggered, did not by any means give way to despair; he busied himself as much as ever with his work on the Committee of Public Instruction, and drew up a report which he printed and distributed in the Convention. The next point for the Committee-men to gain was the expulsion of Cloots from the Convention itself. Needless to say, Cloots had published a conclusive reply to the accusations of Robespierre, but this did not hinder the agents of the Committee from repeating these accusations in journals which were in their pay, with every fresh colouring which malice could devise. The view was now openly put forward that deputies who were by birth foreigners ought to be no longer allowed to take part in the proceedings of the Legislature. In his Appel au genre Humain, perhaps the most brilliant of his pamphlets which he now gave to the world, he reviewed the whole of his public career from the beginning of the Revolution. It was all of no avail. On the fifth of the month, Nivose, Robespierre himself was in the tribune of the Convention, reading a report of the Committee on the principles of Revolutionary Government. "It is the function of Constitutional Government," he said, "to conserve: it is the function of Revolutionary Government to found." For the first time the doctrines of the Robespierrean despotism were formulated from the tribune of the Convention. Robespierre proceeded to justify the necessity of a strong executive by comparing the State to a vessel sailing between two rocks, Moderation on the one hand and Excess on the other. Turning towards Anacharsis he said,

"The two extremes meet. Nothing so much resembles the apostle of federalism and disintegration as the unseasonable preacher of the 'Republic, one and universal.' The friend of kings and the advocate-general of the Human Race understand each other sufficiently well."

Anacharsis turned pale with indignation as he heard the same calumnies he had so thoroughly refuted in the Appel and elsewhere, being served up again for the delectation of his enemies without the slightest hint of their truth ever having been called in question. Robespierre continued to develop his theory of an organised foreign conspiracy in Paris, of which he professed to hold the threads. Barère followed in the same strain, finishing by demanding that all foreigners should be prohibited henceforth from speaking or voting in the Convention. This motion was carried practically without any further discussion, and thus Cloots just found himself for a second time the victim of a carefully-woven plot of the Robespierre-Barère conspiracy.

Two days later Anacharsis with an abstracted air might have been seen walking briskly past the Place de la Revolution, where stood the ominous instrument of the Terror. He stood for a moment and then passed on at an increased pace into the Champs

Elysées. His gloomy forebodings as to his fate were suddenly checked by the sight of two little children sitting by the side of the road and spelling out the words of a school-book. His eyes suddenly filled with tears; he seized the children and covered them with kisses. His work then had not all been in vain! That education, without which true freedom was impossible, and which he had had his share in bringing within reach of the young, would bear its fruit yet! For a few moments he forgot everything but his faith in the future of mankind, though as he returned past the Place de la Revolution towards his own residence in the Hotel de Brionne, the thought of the Committees and of the scoundrel who was conspiring to destroy all that for him made the Revolution worth having and worth living for, can hardly fail to have overwhelmed him again. That same evening he was arrested under a mandate issued by the Committee of General Security – a mandate which coupled his name with that of Thomas Paine.

The Royalist and Robespierreist journals brutally crowed over the fall of Cosmopolitanism in the person of the "Orator of the Human Race," and the triumph of French Chauvinism. The Parisian Sans-Culottists, the Hébertists headed by the Cordeliers Club with its branches throughout the country, rose up in indignation at the incarceration of their leaders – for Ronsin and Vincent had also been arrested. The Declaration of the "Rights of Man," hung up in the hall of the Cordeliers, was veiled with a black cloth emblematic of the displeasure of the popular party at the conduct of the Committees, conduct which they incorrectly attributed principally to the influence of the Dantonist party, who had for some time past been vehemently agitating in favour of the abolition of Revolutionary Government, and of "Moderation" generally. So threatening did matters become, that the Committees were forced by pressure of public opinion and the dread of imminent insurrection to release Ronsin and Vincent, and to promise to release Cloots and others within a few days. Negotiations between the Sans-Culottists and the Government were carried on through the Cordeliers Club, the Commissioner Collet d'Herbois who had recently returned from the provinces, and been added to the Committee of Public Safety, serving as go-between. The matter took on more or less the complexion of a quarrel between two great clubs, the Dantonists and the party of the Government preponderating at the Jacobins. At last the Cordeliers were beguiled by promises, for the fulfilment of which they neglected to obtain any guarantees, into removing the veil from the Declaration of the "Rights of Man," and communicating this fact to the departments. The Robespierreist league now pulled itself together. On the night of the twentieth of Nivose, in direct contravention of the pledges given to the Cordeliers, the matter was decided in full Committee, and Fouquier Tinville, the public prosecutor, summoned to receive orders. Hébert, Vincent, Ronsin, Momoro, were decreed accused, as a first instalment in the holocaust of Sans-Culottism. In vain the Cordeliers protested. The Government had succeeded in inspiring the partizans of Sans-Culottism with panic. In a few days all the leaders who had been in tile van of the revolutionary movement were under lock and key. Most were taken to the Conciergerie, but Ronsin and some others were sent to join Anacharsis Cloots at St. Lazare. Meanwhile the Committee-men and their partizans among the Jacobins began with increased fury to pour forth their deluge of calumnies against the prisoners now deprived of all means of defence. It was even hoped by their friends that in the very absurdity of the accusations levelled against them lay their best hope of acquittal. The masses of the populace were sought to be appeased by statements industriously circulated that the destruction of Sans-Culottism and the "nationalising" of the Revolution meant the return of peace, and the end of the privations they were then suffering from famine.

Fouquier Tinville, who had been fairly staggered at the task assigned him, and who found the difficulties of drawing up any plausible act of accusation against men whose zeal and devotion to the cause of the Revolution were so notorious, to exceed even his powers, was constantly resorting to the Committee for guidance. Robespierre now hit upon the plan made famous in the later period of the Terror, that namely of consolidating the indictment of a number of persons into one act of accusation. This was the first case in which the above procedure was adopted. The prisoners to be arraigned in the present trial were composed chiefly, though not entirely, of the party of the Commune, i.e., of the Cordeliers Society, a few nondescript shades of Moderatism being dexterously included. It was on the first of Germinal that the accused, nineteen by the tale, were brought before the Revolutionary Tribunal. Amongst them was the Dutch banker, De Kock, father of the novelist Paul de Kock, who besides having helped to found the propagandist journal Le Batave, had devoted an enormous fortune to the support of the armies and the cause of the Revolution generally. It was at his house in the environs of Paris that Hébert, Anacharsis and other leaders of Sans-Culottisrn used frequently to meet for friendly discussion. Anacharsis and some of the others still believed in the integrity of the jury, but Ronsin and Vincent saw that a terrorism had been set up which rendered all chance of escape hopeless.

The accusations, vague enough, were supported by depositions of an equally ridiculous character. Every time anything was said which might tell in favour of the prisoners, or which might implicate other persons whom it was not convenient to prosecute, the witnesses were promptly cut short by the president, Dumas. Cloots, although included in the general indictment of having conspired to overthrow the Republic in the interests of Royalism and of the foreign powers, was but little referred to individually in the course of the proceedings. The only fact that was seriously alleged against him was that he had some months before, out of good-nature, endeavoured to procure the liberation of a woman who was in prison as a suspect. The trial lasted in all three days, and thirty-six witnesses were heard. The last day the public galleries were crowded with Moderates of all shades, with Robespierreists and with Jacobin partizans of the Committee, who howled down the accused the moment they attempted to say anything in their defence, and hailed every accusation with cries of "To the guillotine." Charged towards the close of the day's proceedings with having treacherously plotted with his theory of a "Universal Republic," Cloots replied:

"Citizens, the Universal Republic is in the system of nature. As for suspecting me to be the partizan of kings merely because I have declared myself the enemy of them all, you dare not do it."

On some dispute occurring between two of his comrades, when the victims were brought back to the prison, Anacharsis conjured them in the name of fraternity in death, like himself, to sleep their last night on earth in the quiet of a good conscience. The following morning they were again brought up before the tribunal, but the proceedings on this occasion were little more than formal. At mid-day they were all declared guilty and sentenced to death without respite. Amidst the declarations of innocence which proceeded from some of the prisoners, the voice of Cloots was heard exclaiming – "I appeal from your sentence to the Human Race, but like Socrates I will drink the hemlock with pleasure." "The Republic is dead," said Hébert to Ronsin. "It is immortal," replied the general.

Late the same afternoon the tumbrils were to be seen forcing their way through dense and disorderly crowds, egged on to every form of insult against the occupants by the partizans of Robespierre, to the Place de la Revolution. Hébert was in the first cart bathed in tears. Cloots was on the last, calm and at times even smiling. The indecent jubilation of the Dantonists, headed by the young journalistic ruffian, Camille Desmoulins, over the downfall of all that was purest and best in the revolutionary movement was not of long duration. Robespierre and the Committee men, in making an end of Sans-Culottisin and the advanced section of Revolutionists, did not intend compromising themselves with the Parisian populace, by getting tarred with the ultra-Moderatism and highly-dangerous, because ill-concealed, intrigues of the Dantonist party. The latter, moreover, were becoming extremely inconvenient to the Government, especially to Robespierre, for while as friends they tended to compromise him with the populace, as enemies they stood in the way of his ambition. They were destined soon to find out the nature of the man whom they had flattered, and who, until quite recently, had professed the warmest friendship for them. He suddenly rounded on them, and in a few days all the chief leaders of the party, including Danton and his lieutenant, Camille, followed the Hébertists to the national scaffold. Both sides alike prophesied that they should be avenged on Robespierre, a prediction which fulfilled itself four months later. Both parties were to Robespierre "unseasonable" (intempestatif) – the first, because by what he deemed their revolutionary excesses, they stood in the way of the diplomatic relations he was endeavouring to establish with the powers, and which he fondly hoped would make him the Washington of France; and because their whole tendency, as exemplified in their drastic application of the law of maximum, was obnoxious to the merchants, shopkeepers, fore-stallers, market-riggers, army-contractors, and middle-classes generally, of whose cause Robespierre had latterly constituted himself the especial champion. The second, if for no other reason, because their importunate demands for what practically amounted to a general amnesty, and the total cessation of the Terror, did not, by any means, fit in with his plans for getting rid of his opponents. But the attempt of the "Incorruptible" to moderate the Revolution by throwing the heads of the leading Revolutionists to the coalition was a conspicuous failure. In spite of the martyrdom of her rebellious son, Prussia did not detach herself from the alliance, and the war continued as before. With the middle-classes at home Robespierre was more successful. The merchants, shop-keepers, fore-stallers, and market-riggers, accepted him, not unwillingly, as their bulwark against Sans-Culottism. He was, at all events for them, the lesser of two evils. As soon as the frontiers were clear, they tossed aside their wretched instrument, who at last reaped the just reward of his toadyism and villainy. Unfortunately, seen through the reaction which followed his fall, this blight and canker of the Revolution had the good fortune to acquire the halo of a doubly false reputation. On the one hand he was abused by reactionary writers as the embodiment of the very thing he attacked, Sans-Culottism, simply because he had not dared to go to the full length of abolishing the maximum, and because in his own personal interest he had systematically abused, for his own purposes, the system which the true Sans-Culottes had been only anxious to use against proven traitors during a period of crisis. On the other side he has been lauded by certain callow rhetoricians and popular political essayists as the incarnation of the "people's cause," because, forsooth, he was followed by reactionists, who found it possible to go greater lengths than he in the work of "moderating" and "nationalising" the Revolution.

William Morris once said to me that he regarded Jean Calvin as "quite the worst man that has ever lived." I would pair with the name of Jean Calvin, in this distinction, that of Maximilien Robespierre. The old French province of Picardy assuredly deserves the merit of having produced, at an interval of two hundred years, two of the most exquisitely developed scoundrels the world has ever seen – Calvin in the 16th, Robespierre in the 18th, century. Both alike were redolent of cant; Calvin sniffed the theological cant of the 16th century, with its Christian bigotry and asceticism; Robespierre the political cant of the 18th century, with its Rousseauite intolerance and affectation of Roman austerity. Both alike were bloodless, bilious, blear-eyed abortions – crosses between the fish and the human – who owed the reputation they gained with simpletons for "clean-living," "purity," and "incorruptibility," in a great measure to this very fact. Shakspere must surely have had these two precious Picards in the view of his prophetic soul when he spoke of the "treacherous, kindless villain." Poor Anacharsis Cloots had the misfortune to fall into the jaws of the second of these monsters, as poor Michael Servet did into those of the first.

The two central ideas for which Anacharsis Cloots lived and suffered martyrdom were those of Internationalism and of Free-Thought. It was Voltaire that gave him his stimulus rather than Rousseau. Willing, though he was, to sacrifice his fortune, and, what is more, willing though he was that the fortune of his class should be sacrificed in the cause of the Revolution, supporter though he was of the drastic application of the maximum with a view of alleviating the miseries of the working-classes during the crisis, as well as of forcible requisitions on the property of the rich for the support of the armies – it is nevertheless plain that he did not appreciate the significance of economics as the cornerstone of historical progress any more than did his equally well-meaning contemporaries, Hébert, Chaumette, Vincent, and the rest. The conception of a classless society, it is evident from various passages in his writings, had not so much as dawned upon him. The only economic ideal he had, was probably that of a system of peasant proprietorship which should ensure a competence for all, combined with a public opinion which should compel the wealthy to voluntarily devote the greater part of their riches to public purposes. This view he held simply because no other had been pointed out to him, and the conditions of contemporary industry did not allow him to see any other. He believed, what well-nigh all thinkers believed before Karl Marx, that the ground-work of historic evolution was political and speculative, rather than social and economic. For him the "universal republic," with Paris, the home of the "new culture," as its Metropolis, in which all distinction of nationality should disappear, and the whole human family should constitute one people – in conjunction with the destruction of supernatural religions, and the establishment on their ruins of an atheistic cultus (as represented by the worship of Reason, having its head-quarters in Paris) – would, he thought, alone suffice to put an end to oppression, misery, and war, and to inaugurate the new era of Liberty, Equality, and Fraternity. These principles he kept steadily before him throughout Ins whole public career, without swerving or compromise of any kind whatever, and for them he sacrificed his energies, his fortune, and finally his life. It was in their interest he unceasingly advocated a war of propaganda which should extend the frontiers of what was ultimately to become the World Republic without delay and as far as possible. He abhorred the notion of the temporary and patched-up peace which the Girondists and the Robespierreists were alike anxious to obtain, at the price of sacrificing to the reactionary powers abroad and to the reactionary classes at home the central principles of the Revolution by reducing it to the proportions of a mere change in the form of French government.

The merit of the "Orator of the Human Race" consists in his having been the first to formulate Cosmopolitanism as a principle, and his having been at least one of the first to insist on the definite abandonment by the people collectively of supernatural creeds and cults as an essential condition of liberty and progress. Before the French Revolution, emancipation from priestcraft and dogma had been the special privilege of the aristocratic and well-to-do classes, a privilege which they were zealous of vindicating for themselves against the "common people," as all eighteenth-century literature bearing upon the subject shows. Free-thought was henceforth to become incorporated in the great popular movement of European progress. Cloots, as already indicated, failed to see that the principles of Internationalism and Rationalism, upon whose connexion with the great revolutionary ideal of popular sovereignty he so justly insisted, had their roots in the existing economic conditions of society. He failed to distinguish between the "third estate" and the "people." For him, as for the vast majority of his contemporaries, there were but two opposed classes – the first represented by kings, priests, and nobles, and the second by all who were not kings, priests, and nobles. The antagonism even between these two classes was for him largely a political one, such economical inequalities as existed being based essentially on political inequality and destined to pass away with the abolition of the latter. He could not see that the political privileges of the first and second estates were simply the sign and seal of a fundamental economical privilege, and that that very "third estate," which. seemed to so many, indeed more or less to all, to have identical interests with the whole of the people, was already constituting itself a privileged class, prepared to step into the place left vacant by the deposition of the feudal classes – and further, that "popular sovereignty," "cosmopolitanism," and the "empire of reason," would only be so far tolerated as they did not compromise the material interests, real or supposed, of the new class – so long as that new class remained the dominant power in the State. But these defects of intellectual vision were incident to the period in which he lived, and do not in any way detract from the interest attaching to our Orator as a typical figure of French Revolutionary life.

What strikes one in him, as in many writers and thinkers of the period, as compared with ourselves in this present century-end, is the singular and almost child like naiveté of his enthusiasm. Our enthusiasm to-day, even when at its highest, is always "sicklied o'er with the pale cast of thought." The century which divides us from the French Revolution has made the world old in a sense in which not even a millennium had done before. As a consequence, what to the mind of the "age of reason," which

43

could see nothing in the future of humanity but the glow of a breaking summer's day, appeared full of life and reality, seems to us often but turgid rhetoric or vapid bombast. Let us think of this when we look back on the martyr-Orator, and we shall forgive him for calling himself the "Orator of the Human Race," for talking about drinking the hemlock with Socrates, and for many another eighteenth-century flourish! We shall none the less honour him as one of the indirect precursors of the working-class movement of modern times, and we shall love him as the single-minded hero and apostle of two great ideas, which will assuredly one day be realised, although not, perhaps, precisely in the manner he expected.

2. The Decay of Pagan Thought

(January 1890)

It is probable that comparatively few educated persons, even in the present day, fully realize the fact that the historical Paganism of the ancient world had a development. They are accustomed to regard the religion of the Homeric age of ancient Greece, with its gods, goddesses, and heroes, as essentially the same with the religion of the Roman Empire in the fourth century after Christ – as the religion, that is, which Constantine renounced, and which Theodosius suppressed. Going on the assumption that the gods of Homer and Hesiod were still worshipped, and the crude popular legends respecting them still believed, where not openly rejected, by even the cultivated inhabitants of the Empire, and that the ancient morality with which these worships were connected, still existed without noteworthy change, these persons not unnaturally regard Christianity as a system embodying a new spirit and code of ideas, theological and ethical, which suddenly burst upon the world, arresting attention by the startling contrast it presented to the prevailing creeds and habits of thought. Their wonder at this marvellous and unprecedented phenomenon is perennial, and furnishes a powerful argument, as they think, for detaching Christianity from the main stream of natural historical development. Now, without unduly trenching upon theological ground, with which we are not here directly concerned, we may readily admit that if the case were as stated; if a totally new view of nature, of man's destiny, and of the aims of his life, had really fallen upon the world without any assignable connexion with previous or current thought, there would certainly have been a plausible case for regarding the Christian religion as something organically distinct from all other creeds and systems, theological and philosophical. The object of the following pages is to state

45

briefly the facts of the case.

The great change which came over the speculative and ethical thought of the world, about the time that the Roman dominion had finally consolidated itself, or which, at least, then first became generally manifest, has been too long neglected by the general historian. Yet, the tremendous and far-reaching significance of this change can hardly be over-estimated, whether we regard it as the condition or symptom of the great transition-period which followed. The struggle between Caesar and Pompey for possession of the world Empire, is itself scarcely so significant an event as the introduction and spread of the introspective spirit, and of the mystical doctrines derived for the most part from the east which was just then beginning. The stern civic virtue of Rome, the devotion entire and complete of the man of antiquity generally to his "city" and his kindred was rapidly sinking to its lowest ebb. The "gods" – the visible sign and symbol of ancient city-life – had, in the case of numberless cities, been transferred to Rome. And what could this mean to the inhabitants, but that their city as an independent, social and political organism, had ceased to exist, that the supreme object of the devotion of their ancestors was gone? The old religion and the old morality in its most sacred form had ceased to be, for them. They were enrolled as Roman citizens perhaps, but what of that? What was Rome to them apart from its character as the metropolis of culture, but the centre of a corrupt tax-gathering oligarchy and of a military despotism which had forcibly imposed itself upon them? Even to the Roman himself, the city with its crowds of strangers, its violent contrasts of rich and poor, and its purchasable citizenship was not the Rome of Quintus Curtius, or of Manlius. The ancient forms of city and of family life and worship still subsisted, it is true, but as dried and mechanical usages from winch the life had fled. The pax Romana, had abolished for the provincial the duty of military service in defence of his city. Its magistracies and functions were

46

reduced to sinecures; its distinctive religion as such was virtually abolished.

Economically a correspondingly great change had takes place. The old independent freeholder, working his land and his domestic slaves for his own behoof, had become almost extinct, – great amalgamated estates called latifundia, worked by armies of slaves under a villius or overseer, and cultivated with a view to the sale of the produce, had become the rule in farming generally, while in manufacture and commerce the principle of large capital and production for profit was similarly applied – to the ruin of ancient art. For generations past, the ancient city-worship had lost its prestige. The meaning of the fire burning on the prytaneum was forgotten. The public festivals, the ancient hymns, had sunk into mere conventional usages for the ordinary man, their investigation only interesting the antiquary. From the time of Sokrates onward, and especially since the conquests of Alexander had broken down the previously existing barriers between Europe and the East, the ancient moral and religious sentiments, whose object was the tribe and the city, and for which the individual as such had no place, had been positively undergoing a negative process of decay from within. It was now being undermined by the notions of independent individuality, or personality, of a transcendent deity, the creator and living power of the universe (as distinct from the old deified ancestors and personified natural objects and powers), and of a higher life of the soul after death. These ideas, which had received the fullest expression in the east, and the morality based on them, in which the categories of sin and holiness have superseded those of civic virtue and its contrary, of justice and injustice, &c., had been for generations steadily gaining the upper hand among the cultivated classes. The Roman imperium in absorbing all the old city-cults merely gave material shape to what was already accomplished in the moral sphere Another and more positive way, in which the world-empire coincided with, and gave a certain expression to, current speculative tendencies, was in the fact of its centralisation. An all-dominant city – a centre from which all power radiated was a fitting analogue of the one ultimate source of all things, of which the inferior gods were only the feeble reflex, to which all religions with their divine rites and ceremonies pointed, and who alone was the true object of worship.

These ideas which, as before remarked, had taken their rise some centuries before Christ, had been slowly and surely permeating the then world, till, about the first century of the Christian era, they had become conspicuous among all classes, and apart from an exception to be presently noticed, dominant among all persons possessing any claim to cultivation. There was a universal tendency to look toward the east, and to the oracles and literatures of past ages and ancient races for the solution of the problems respecting the soul's relation to the supreme divine power and its destiny after death. The cults and literatures of the oriental world were supposed to enshrine this, and various mysteries and secret rites sprang up, having for their object the setting forth by the aid of symbolism, traditional and fantastic, esoteric doctrines concerning God, immortality, &c.

In considering the intellectual and religious aspect of the expiring world of antiquity, it is important to bear in mind the peculiarly fluid nature of ancient religious conceptions. The world of personified natural forces and objects which, in conjunction with the world of ancestral spirits, constituted for the ancients the field of religious thought and observance, was always vague and shadowy. Its several figures tended sometimes to coalesce and sometimes to separate, wreathing themselves into the most varied combinations. Even the distinction between ancestral hero and personified natural force or object did not count for much. Time ancestral hero was often also a sun-god, e.g., Herakles. The ancient was ready to see in every foreign divinity that was not obviously tribal or local, another aspect or name of some native nature-god. The essentially magical nature of early religion, of which the varied cults of the Ionian Empire were a survival, must also not be lost sight of. The question of names was of the utmost importance. Every divinity was supposed to have a true, sacred, or esoteric name of wondrous potency, and when invoked by this name, was bound to respond. In the "mysteries" the true name of the divinity was revealed. In addition to this religious magic, the whole of daily life was interpenetrated with a belief in amulets, charms, and sorcery generally, to an extent which might seem incredible to anyone not conversant with the literature of the time. In fact, the whole intellectual atmosphere of antiquity, and especially of the period before us, is one which it is almost impossible for any modern to fully enter into, try as he may, and let his historical perception be never so keen. To take a single instance only. One of the most important cults of antiquity was the solar cult in its various aspects. Yet how did the man of antiquity represent to himself the relations of the several objects of these cults? Did he regard them as diverse aspects of one sun-god, or were they conceived each as a separate personality? Was the "most high God," i.e., the Sun-god as worshipped by the ancient Phoenician at its meridian distinguished by him from the Baal of fertility, the ripening sun-god? Was this again distinct from the Sun-god as symbolising the scorching or the putrefying power of the solar rays (Baal-zebub)? Again, how did the Graeco-Roman regard Apollo and Helios or Sol respectively? Was the distinction one of name only, or was the personality implied in the solar disc distinct from the personality of the god Apollo? Did Khu-nat-en (Amenophis IV.) the Pharaoh who introduced the worship of the visible sun, regard this as distinct from Ra, or only as a new aspect of Ra? These are questions very difficult to answer as regards the earlier ages of Pagan thought, the nearest solution being probably that the question never distinctly presented itself to the ancient mind; but we may affirm with confidence that, at the period under consideration, that of its decline, the tendency was to regard all diversity of name and cult as external and local, and to view the objects of all the leading worships of the Empire as different modes of approaching the same central fact – the one divinity, immanent in, or transcending, the visible world, according to the view of the worshipper. Still, the old confusion lingered on to a great extent in popular conception, till Paganism flickered finally out in the sixth century, nay, lingers on in the different local cults of the "virgin" to this day. To how many a pilgrim to Loretto, St. Jago di Compostella, Mariazell, Einsiedeln, &c., does not the local image enshrine a "virgin" special to itself, and having only a very general connexion with those of other similar establishments.

We have spoken of an exception to the general mystical tendency of' thought throughout the empire. From the time of Augustus onwards till about the end of the second century, there was a movement of thought observable among the literary class, in many cases associated with the philosophy of Epicurus, but also with that of the Sceptics, which ran counter to the prevailing mystical syncretism, and which is reflected in the works of Cicero, Lucretius, Lucian, &c. Though the existence of this movement is unquestionable, its importance has been undoubtedly exaggerated by many historians who, like Gibbon, have assumed it to have been co-extensive with the whole of the educated classes. This it could never have been, even when at its zenith in the Augustan age, and it soon after declined, till in the third century there are scarcely any more traces of it left. The mystical movement which was going on alongside of it eventually swallowed it up. It may be doubted, indeed, whether at any time it extended beyond a few of the principal centres. The rationalism of antiquity was at no period more than skin-deep. The mythologic magical theory of nature with which all society was imbued, derived straight from the primitive ideas of pre-historic times, with the modifications induced by altered conditions of culture but still essentially the same, was too powerful to yield to the fitful flashes of the critical spirit. These did not suffice even to weaken, much less to eradicate it.

It is curious to observe how new ideas and principles invariably on their first appearance assume the guise of the old ones with which they are formally in conflict. The early Protestant sects (the Lutherans, the Anabaptists of Munster, &c) retained much of the Catholic cultus, and not a few of the Catholic dogmas; the Catholic ideal of the Christian church as a divine kingdom on earth gave way by no means at once to the essentially Protestant notion of religion as a personal matter. The new philosophy of the Renaissance which attacked Scholasticism, retained, nevertheless, the scholastic manner of approaching problems and the scholastic modes of expression. The dawning physical science of the sixteenth century was steeped in the conceits of magic, alchemy and astrology, as may readily be seen from the writings of such men as Paracelsus, Trithemius, Agrippa, Cardanus. The rising middle-classes, or that section of them which represented commercial interests, up to Adam Smith's time, sought their advantage not in the free competition which is the real soul of commercial. enterprise, but in the old notion of status as embodied in guilds and monopolies. The modern Secularist, whose creed is professedly a protest against church and chapel, nevertheless has his regular Sunday lecture or service after the approved pattern. Even the architecture of the dissenting chapel is maintained; in places where the body is wealthy, the lecture-hall resembling nothing so much as a modern congregationalist church. Instances might be multiplied without number showing that at first it is only in one or two definite points of conflict that new tendencies differentiate themselves from the old, and that the consequences latent in these tendencies are but dimly visible to their early advocates. It is only after having passed through this early development that they begin to become concrete and show what they are in themselves. Thus it was to all appearance with early Christianity. To the eye

51

of the contemporary Pagan it was, barring one or two peculiarities which he might easily trace to its Judaic origin, little if at all distinguishable from the various other "mysteries" then in vogue. They all had certain common characteristics secrecy of initiation, the wearing of special robes, generally white, by the neophyte; the passing through sundry stages of probation, &c., &c. They all professed to offer solutions of the problem of the relation of the soul to its supreme source, and of its destiny after death. With the third century Paganism had visibly undergone a fundamental change. Long before, the current monotheistic tendencies had received an expression in the official religion which planted the worship of the Roman Jupiter Optimus Maximus (J.O.M.) everywhere throughout the length and breadth of the Empire, identifying him with the principal god of every district, with the great Syrian sun-god of Baalbek (J.O.M. Heliopolitanus) no less than with the local divinity of the St. Bernard pass (J.O.M. Poeninus). But this personification of the Roman power was not in essence the kind of monotheism to satisfy a mystical and introspective age such as the second, and still more the third century. The notion of individual holiness, of immortality, of the "other world," of the supra-sensible, was everywhere dominant in men's minds, and what was required was a creed which would embrace this, and formulate it satisfactorily.

The earlier Paganism had only regarded the future life of the soul as a shadow-life, a powerless, objectless dream-existence Only a few specially select heroes were permitted the reward of the Elysian fields or the islands of the blest, which was perhaps never regarded as much more than a poetical fancy. The oriental theory of transmigration was only held by the learned. But with the decline of the ancient Paganism which had its centre in the social organization (clan, tribe, city) on this side the grave, and to which the after life of the individual was a matter of little importance – the doctrine of the Elysian fields and the Happy islands became increasingly popular, and was extended to all respectable persons. This is shown by the sarcophagi and monumental inscriptions of the period.[1] On many of the former, figures of tritons and nereids are to be seen carrying the souls of the departed ones to the "islands of the blest," while numberless inscriptions expressly testify to the devout Pagan's "glorious hope of immortality." Thus we read,

"Ye unhappy living, Bewail this death; but ye gods and goddesses, rejoice at your new fellow-citizen."

"Now for the first thou livest thy happy time, far from all earthly fortune; in heaven on highest thou enjoyest nectar and ambrosia with the gods."

An inscription to a little girl of eight years old runs:

"Ye adored souls of the pious, lead the innocent Magnilla through the Elysian plains to your abodes."

On the grave of an infant is written:

"My heavenly and divine soul will not pass to the land of shades; the universe and the stars will take me up; the earth has only received my body, the stone my name."

A son prays for his father;

"Ye gods of the underworld, open for my father the plains, where, rosy-bright, dawns an eternal day."[2]

The notion of intercession with the gods by deceased persons for their friends below also appears on sundry inscriptions. Aronobius, a Christian writer of the fourth century, refers (Adversus Gentes, ii., p.86) to the belief as general among contemporary Pagans that a happy futurity was the reward of a moral life.

The older mysteries (Samothrakian, Eleusinian, the Bacchanalian, etc.), though still the same as ever outwardly, were undoubtedly furnished with content changed in accordance with changed speculative conditions. We are here chiefly interested in the new mysteries, the object of initiation into which was avowedly the attainment of higher knowledge regarding the relations of the soul to the divinity, and its purification from material impulses, with a view to immortality. The first to notice in this connexion are the Hekate mysteries, which, although they existed previously, now obtained a special notoriety and popularity. There is little known respecting them, literature being wholly silent on the subject, and our only information coming from inscriptions. As is well-known, Hekate herself, the goddess of the underworld, was commonly confounded with Artemis (Diana), Proserpina, the Moon, etc. In the inscriptions of the later period this mystery appears as one of the important cults side by side with those of Mithras, and of the "Great Mother," of which we shall have occasion to speak directly. At Hermannstadt in Hungary there is a bas relief representing the various grades of initiation in the Hekate cultus. Diocletian is said to have erected a Hekate temple at Antioch, to which 365 steps led down, and it would appear that the initiation always took place underground. The cultus of Sabazios the Phrygian Bacchus, extended far and wide throughout the empire. The ordinary ritual of the Sabazios worship was of the usual oriental type comprising chanting, the clashing of cymbals and the beating of drums, as the accompaniment of the wild Phrygian dance. Among the secret rites were comprised the donning of it stag's skin, sprinkling with milk and other purifications, the whole terminating with the mystic and somewhat banal words, "I fled the evil and I found the good." In the third century new rites came to be added, such as the passing of a golden serpent through the clothes of the neophyte (ostensibly in memory of the loves of Zeus and Demeter), who was then introduced into the sanctum when he was required to repeat the words, "I have eaten from the tambourine, I have drunken from the cymbal, now I am initiated," and sundry other apparently meaningless formulas. The later Christian writers saw in the snake an evidence of the direct participation of the devil in the proceedings.

More direct evidence of the drift of the mysteries is afforded by those of the "mother of the gods," the mysterious divinity who was identified with the "Syrian goddess," whose great temple was at Hierapolis, and of whom Lucian has left so graphic a description; and also with Kybele, Urania, Rhea, & as, being in fact sometimes styled the "goddess of many names." The new mysteries which were now composed on the older elements of the Phoenician or Phrygian cult centred in the ritual of the Taurobolia which were introduced in Rome from the East about the time of the Antonines, and consisted in the sacrifice of a bull and sometimes of a ram (Kriobolia). The neophyte claimed on the completion of the ceremony to be "re-born to all eternity" (in aeternum renatus). The initiations into these "mysteries" in Rome itself took place on the hill of the Vatican, the customary hour for this celebration being midnight. A deep fosse was made in the ground, and covered with planks, which had been bored through, and formed it kind of sieve. The neophyte arrayed in symbolical clothing and ornaments was placed in the fosse. The sacrifices were made on the top, and the neophyte, as the blood of the victim flowed through the apertures, sought to bathe himself in it – to catch as much of it as possible on his face, hair, and dress. It was through this washing in the blood of the lamb or the bull that he acquired his regeneration. He became a taurobolus. But the initiation was not completed by the ceremony alone. To be sure of his salvation he had to wear the Blood-stained garments for a specified time afterwards, and to expose himself to all the contumely which might befall him in consequence. The notion of purification by blood is constantly appearing in the Pagan "mysteries" of the empire. One of the initiated into the Taurobolia, a prefect of the city of Rome, and proconsul of Africa, seriously thanks the gods that his soul is now safe.

The mysteries of Isis formed another of the chief refuges for the subject of the emperor who was in distress respecting his soul's welfare. The immediate object of the Isis mysteries was the representation of the mutilation of Osiris and the recovery of the lost fragments. This had become overlaid in the imperial age by a mass of mystical and esoteric lore, mainly dealing with the doctrine of personal immortality. The processions and representations, which formed part of the initiating ceremonies, are said to have had as their object to symbolize death, and resurrection by the grace of Isis. By this time Isis had, of course, become mixed up with Proserpine, Here, and other divinities. Respecting the mysterious signs and prodigies, vouchsafed to the neophyte during his initiation, the words of Lucius give some idea:

"I passed through the gates of death, I trod the threshold of Proserpine, and after I had ridden through all elements I returned. At midnight I saw the sun in its fullest splendour. I approached the gods of the upper and the under-world and I adored them in their presence."

We can only guess at the nature of the spectacle presented to the eyes of the initiated, and whether the sights and sounds that appealed to his awestruck senses were due to mechanical contrivances or hypnotism or what not, we have no means of determining.

The Eleusinian rites, though exclusively local, were an important element in the religious life of the decaying world of antiquity. All who could afford, and who were possessed with the Zeitgeist, travelled to Greece to become initiated into these most ancient and famous of all the mysteries of the Greek-speaking world. The Eleusinian ritual had in all probability attained its completed form at a much earlier period than the other mystical cults. In this, as presumably in the other "mysteries," of which we have less full accounts, the processes of initiation were long and exhausting, involving severe fasts, penances and religious exercises. The Eleusinian aspirant began his noviciate in February, with the so-called lesser mysteries at Athens. He was admitted a Mystes at Eleusis the following September, but he had to wait another twelvemonth before he could enter in the final stage of his initiation. Previous to doing so, a nine days' fast had to be very carefully observed, during which prescribed religious exercises were fulfilled. Then came the initiation in the temple itself, which consisted in an elaborate and gorgeous spectacle listened to in devout silence. At last the votary was allowed to see, handle, and taste, the sacramental objects and to pronounce the mysterious formula. A recent writer has observed that a modern Greek church on the eve of Easter Sunday may convey some idea of the scene.

But more than all the "mysteries" hitherto described, those of Mithras attained the most wide-spread popularity, during the third and fourth centuries. The worship of the Persian Mithras, originally the God of daylight (the Mitra of the Vedas), but subsequently under Zoroastrianism, the chief sun-god, was introduced into the Roman Empire by the Cilician pirates about

57

B.C. 80. The secret cultus, however, did not receive full official sanction till A.D. 100. From this time it became an increasingly powerful factor in the religious life of the Roman world till its final suppression, in the year 376, by Theodosius.

The Mithraic rites seem to have varied little from their first introduction into the empire. Though all or most of the mysteries had many points in common with the noviciate of the Christians, there is none in which the likeness is so marked as in the Mithraic.

"The principal rites of the worship of Mithras," says the late Mr. King (The Gnostics and their Remains, p.122), "have a very curious resemblance to those subsequently established in the Catholic Church ... The Neophytes were admitted by the rite of Baptism the initiated at their assemblies solemnly celebrated a species of Eucharist; whilst the courage and endurance of the candidate for admission into the sect were tested by twelve consecutive trials called the 'tortures,' undergone within a cave constructed for the purpose; all which tortures had to be passed through before participation in the mysteries was granted to the aspirant."

Many of the contemporary Gnostic sects undoubtedly drew much from Mithraism, which is also the ultimate source of much of the cryptic lore of the secret societies of the middle ages and of modern times. As in the case of many other ancient cults, the follower of Mithras was indicated by a mystic mark or sign on the forehead, (cf., "the mark of the beast.") The Mithraic Eucharist was celebrated with water and bread in a manner precisely similar to the Christian.

The bread used was a round cake, emblematic of the solar disc and called Mizd, a name in which some scholars see the origin of the word missa, as designating the sacrifice of the mass, the cake of which is precisely similar in form. During the Mithraic probation of forty days, it is alleged, the aspirant lay naked for several nights on snow and was afterwards scourged for the space of two days. In the museum at Innsbruck are to be seen certain Mithraic tablets on which are portrayed the twelve tests of initiation. Large numbers of Mithraic inscriptions and amulets have been preserved, many of which indicate the horrors of initiation; besides the lying in snow and the scourging, terrors of all kinds (the original of modern masonic "apprentice" rites) stretchings upon a Procrustean bed, contact with fire, fastings in the wilderness, &c., &c. Several distinct degrees of initiation are mentioned, which seem to have been ranged in series of triplets. After the primary initiation the first grade was that of warrior of Mithras, which was followed by the lion and the bull. They were the lower or earthly grades. The candidate then passed through the grades which belonged to the region of Ather, those of the vulture, the ostrich and the raven respectively. He then reached the sphere of pure fire, through the grades of Griphon, Perses and the Sun. Last of all complete union with the divine nature was attained, through. the grades of father eagle, father and father of fathers. Even he who had attained the lowest grade, that of warrior, was supposed to consider himself separate from the world. It is alleged by Tertullian that when offered a laurel crown, as for example, at any festivity, he was to repudiate it with the words, "My crown is Mithras." The rites of the Mithras cultus were performed in a sacred cave on the side of a hill. Several of these caves have been discovered at various places, including the Roman military stations on the Pauian and Rhaetian frontier. They vary in dimensions, many of them being quite small. The Mithraic ritual obviously did not involve gorgeous dramatic representations such as the Eleusinian and other ancient mysteries, being doubtless externally altogether simple in character, though the great Mithras cave or temple on the

Capitoline hill at Rome, which was destroyed in 378 by order of Theodosius, must have been of some pretensions, as was probably the case with others in the larger towns of the empire. There are few more numerous remains of the religious life of the last ages of antiquity than the dedicatory inscriptions to Deo Solis Invictae Mithrae. The usual figure represents Mithras performing the mystic sacrifice at the shrine; a young man in flowing robes is seen kneeling on a bull, one hand seizing its head and the other plunging a sword into its neck. A dog, a snake, and a scorpion are drinking the blood which flows from the wound. A raven is seated on a rock beside Mithras. The sun (Phoebus), the moon, (Luna), and seven stars, probably representing the seven Persic archangels, the sacred fires, &c., also figure in many Mithraic talismans. That Mithras soon absorbed Apollo, Helios and all other solar deities goes without saying. But of the fusion Mithras with other divinities we shall have more to say presently. The subject of Mithraic Symbolism is fairly exhausted in King's Gnostics, pp.114-17.

Rivalling the worship of Mithras in popularity and diffusion among the Pagan population of the Roman Empire was that of Serapis, the celebrated statue of whom was brought over from Sinope to Alexandria by order of Ptolemy Soter in the 3rd century B.C. The God of Pontus soon became identified as the god of the dead with the Egyptian Osiris (osiris-apis), and later of course with Jupiter and a crowd of other divinities. The great statue and temple in Alexandria constituted one of the wonders of the world. The Serapeum reared its collossal structure above every other building of the great city. A flight of a hundred steps raised the entrance above the ground. Within, the gigantic statue of the god, composed of all the precious metals plated together, towered up to the roof, and with its outstretched arms touched either side of the great central hall. The Serapeum contained numerous passages and special apartments, while underneath was the great library. If many Christian practices are to be found in

Mithraicism, perhaps still more are discoverable in Serapeanism. The first we hear of the monastic life is in connexion with the worship of Serapis, the Alexandrian temple itself containing numerous cells for those who intended devoting themselves to serving the God by a life of abstinence. Later on, the Christians formed their ascetic establishments on the precise model of these. The temple was famous for its great "functions," in which awe-inspiring "miracles" were displayed. The building must have been fitted up with numerous mechanical appliances for producing spectacular effects, including the celebrated brazen disc of the sun floating in mid-air. The sick were supposed to secure their recovery by advice given in a dream sent by the God in the temple of Aesculapius. Besides the Serapeum itself, the whole of Alexandria was full of shrines, pillars, and other monuments to the great God.

The cultus of Serapis, more than any other of the contemporary religions, succeeded in inspiring a certain awe, if not actual acknowledgment, on the part of the Christians. In a remarkable letter of the Emperor Hadrian, preserved by the historian Vopisend, it is stated that

"those who worship Serapis are also Christians, even such as call themselves Bishops of Christ being devoted to Serapis. The patriarch himself when he comes to Egypt is forced by some to worship Serapis, by others Christ. One God exists for all, and Him do Christians, Jews, and Gentiles worship."

This is interesting, not merely as showing the loose and shifting character of the Christian religion even in the second century, but as illustrating the then orthodox attitude of men of culture on the subject of religion. It has been remarked, as bearing on the above quotation, that the conventional portrait of

61

the founder of Christianity bears so strong a resemblance to the majestic head of the Serapis as to lead to the inference that it was borrowed from the latter. In any case, the relations between the Church and the worship of Serapis would seem to have been exceptional, since, as is well known, it was the last of the great Pagan cults to be overthrown, many of the Christians dreading that any violence to the sacred image would involve the destruction of heaven and earth. The fall of Serapis gave the coup de grace to Paganism in the cities. If the great Serapis could be thrown down and trampled under foot with impunity, it was obvious that the old Gods were one and all impossible any longer as objects of worship. The spirit animating the ancient religion had to satisfy itself henceforth with images of the Virgin and saints, and with relic-worship, which, from this time (the end of the 4th century), began to progress by leaps and bounds.

It would hardly be too much to say that Mithras and Serapis were the only Gods with which the educated Pagan seriously concerned himself from the middle of the third century onwards. The old Graeco-Roman divinities, the Gods of Olympus, and of the Pantheon, continued still in art and literature and in official ceremonies, but they failed to secure the real devotion of the average cultured inhabitant of the cities. Everything tended towards a Pantheism in which the sun, the source of life and light as personified, was regarded as the highest visible expression of the divine, and with it Mithras and often Serapis were identified, the older official gods being in their turn identified with these. With this solar worship that of the moon, as Isis, the consort of the sun, was often united. For those of a more reflective turn, the visible sun was of course only the manifestation and symbol of the great spiritual power of the universe. Such probably represents, as nearly as possible, the state of mind of the average man of education, the citizen of Rome, of Alexandria, Nicomedia, Ephesus, Antioch, during the third and fourth centuries. It is the view, moreover, expressly adopted by Julian in his essay on the sovereign Sun. The great part which solar worship played in all the ancient religions of the East, which had for long been the most popular worships throughout the Empire, naturally contributed to the spread of this Pan-Solism. That Baal, Amen-Ra, Mithras, Serapis, Dionysus, Apollo, Jupiter, were different forms in which the Sovereign deity, the Sun, embodied himself at different times and places as the object of worship among men, became the prevalent notion. The attachment of the later Pagan Emperors to solar worship is well known. Eliobalus sought to make the Syrian Baal worship the supreme cultus of the empire. Aurelian was untiring in erecting temples and altars to the Sun. Even Constantine, after his supposed conversion, was with good reason suspected throughout his life of secret attachment to Sun worship; all his coins are inscribed on the reverse with the figure of time sun and the words dei solis invicti. That this was the case with other less distinguished converts from Paganism there can be little doubt. But if the more important Deities were resolved by the later Pagan into personifications of the Sun, the countless host of divinities – gods and goddesses – of the second, third, and fourth rank became increasingly regarded as mere daimonii, whom it was necessary to worship and propitiate as vice-gerents of the supreme power, and as possessing a legitimate place in the divine hierarchy, but not as heretofore ruling by their own right. The transition from this to angel and saint-worship was obviously easy. The writings of Proclus, the last great Pagan theologian, which formulate this view of the Pagan side, were adopted bodily by the pseudo-Dionysius and in the form of his treatise became the basis of the mediaeval catholic theology.

The above leads us to the consideration of the two leading currents of doctrine – the one philosophic and the other quasi-philosophic – which went on pari passu, with the rise and progress of the Neo-Paganism. The first-mentioned, the mystical reaction against the previous scepticism, is directly traceable to the influence of oriental thought and of the mystical tendencies of the age reacting on the older Greek philosophies, especially that of the Pythagoreans and of Plato. Of the Neo-Cynics, who professed no doctrine beyond that of the "simplification of life," otherwise expressed, Asceticism, it is only necessary to make mention, as showing the tendency of current thought on its practical side. The doctrines which received their final form in the Neo-Platonic philosophy all turned upon the freeing of the soul from the imperfections of sense and its union with the divinity. The soul in its mundane state is burdened with the ignorance and guilt of sensible matter. The aim of the philosopher is to free his soul from sense, and raise it as a purely intelligible essence to oneness with the supreme intelligence whence all things flow. The pure intelligible principle is blurred and confounded by the essential nothingness and falsehood of sense. At first, the emancipation of intellect from sense was conceived as attainable by reason, but later on only by a mystical ecstasy or internal illumination. Such was the theoretical basis of the movement in question. It was the philosophic formulation of the problems then occupying men's attention.

The parallel and more avowedly theosophical movement – that of Gnosticism – was an amalgam of the oriental cults, chiefly those of Babylonia and Persia, with a clash of Platonism, various Judaeo-Christian notions, especially that of an atoning Messiah, being incorporated. Here everything was personified – the freeing of the soul from the impurities and the bondage of sense and matter was to be accomplished by the possession of the gnosis or true knowledge which was revealed to the elect by the redeeming Aeon or Christ, who, issuing from the highest God, became incarnate for the purpose of restoring the human soul, immersed in matter, to its native purity. The manner of this incarnation was one of the points of distinction between the various systems, as also the position and function of the series of beings or Aeons (apparently conceived as in a way existent in time and space) which formed the intermediate links between the lowest principle or world of matter, and the highest principle, "the unspeakable God." In the fourth century the system of Manes (circa 214-278), with its Zoroastrian doctrine of the perennial opposition of a good and evil principle, spread widely and absorbed much of the older Gnosticism. We refrain from entering in further detail into the various phases of neo-pythagorean or neo-platonic and gnostic thought, familiar as they are to everyone who has ever opened a church history or a history of philosophy. Those who failed to find the Pagan cults and mysteries, with their fragmentary doctrines, alone satisfying as a solution of the problems which disturbed them, thought they discovered a more complete and systematic theory of the universe as regards the dominant categories of sin and holiness, good and evil, "light and darkness," in Neoplatonism or Gnosticism as the case might be. The more thoughtful and cultivated man naturally chose the philosophical theory, the less cultivated and more impulsive and superstitious, the semi-mythological one. Meanwhile the Christian Church gathered volume, and attained precision in its doctrine from its trituration with these various sects, unconsciously assimilating some of their theories, consciously opposing itself to others, but always remaining distinct as an organization, till its elevation by Constantine to supremacy over the moral and intellectual life of the Roman world, from which time it was safe from serious disintegration.

Yet another influence which was developing itself simultaneously with the development of Neo-Paganism, Neo-Platonism and Gnosticism throughout the second, third, and fourth centuries was the enormous spread of magical practices and the concurrent rise of astrology as a distinct belief. It was not only a concern for the future life which animated the denizen of the Empire. This world also assumed a new and mysterious aspect. The orthodox and official ceremonies and sacrifices were looked upon as antiquated and flat, and refuge was increasingly sought for in new and strange charms. Every difficulty was sought to be got over, every wish to be fulfilled by means of amulets and incantations. Sorcery of course had existed from the earliest times, and laws had frequently been enacted against it, especially against injury to agricultural property (blighting of crops, &c.) by magical means, but in early times, save for the public religious exercises of the community, which of course partook of a magical character, it was an exceptional thing. Now, on the other hand, the public exercises were held of small account, and private magic became the order of the day. Astrology had also existed as the peculiar function of the Chaldeans from a very early period, but in the Graeco-Roman world, at least, it did not attain any great importance till the time of which we are treating. Now astrologers, no less than magicians, were consulted by all, and were generally to be found permanently installed in the households of the wealthy. What was before merely a sporadic phenomenon of ancient social life now became a part of its daily round.

The issue of every undertaking, unimportant no less that important, was sought to be ascertained by the stars. Disease was treated by charms; enemies sought to be destroyed by incantations. Amulets were worn by all. The gems and charms of this period are well-known to antiquaries. The enormous fame and following of such wonder-workers as Apollonius of Tyana, Peregrinus and Alexander of Abnotichos in the first and second centuries, will give us some idea of what was going on on a smaller scale all over the empire – in every city and village – until the final fall of Paganism. The prevailing cults and philosophies had all of them their necromantic side, or their theory of magic. As a matter of course, Christianity absorbed this tendency. The miracles of saints, the magical powers of relics, of the sign of the cross, the invocation of Christian sacred names, the repetition of paternosters and aves in course of time superseded the more obviously Pagan magic of the fourth century. The ease with which the ancient creed was suppressed and the rapidity with which the Christian swelled its ranks after its official establishment, show not only the moribund character of the Pagan forms, but how the difference between the two had become merely a question of names and external rites. The epistle of the Emperor Julian exhorting the Pagan priesthood to set an example to their adherents of sobriety of life, &c., might easily have been the encyclical of a Christian metropolitan. The worship previously accorded to Isis was now given to the Virgin, the same black images, some of which exist to this day, doing duty in the new role.

From this short sketch, which might be indefinitely expanded on various sides, it will be evident to any unprejudiced mind that Christianity ultimately became the highest embodiment of a movement of which at first it was merely the symptom, and to the expression of which it could originally lay no exclusive claim. The germs of this movement were already present before it. Other expressions of introspective individualism and mysticism developed independently and alongside of Christianity, and to this it was indebted for many of its doctrines and ceremonies. The religion and philosophy of the ancient world went out in a creed which it had itself helped to build up. In the fourth century, as the late Mr. King well observes in a note to his translation of Gregory Nazianzen's invective[3], the state of the empire under Julian resembled that of England under Mary (and he might have added of other countries also during the latter half of the 16th century.)

"The new religion," he observes, "in each case was held by a small minority, but well-organised and extremely noisy; the rest of the population, except in certain districts where local causes kept up zeal for the ancient religion, were entirely

67

indifferent to principles, but eager for the plunder of the temple lands and treasures, as of those of the abbeys and cathedrals. This state of things clearly appears from Julian's complaints in the Mistopagon."

Thus economical causes combined, with political and speculative, to ensure the success of the new creed.

The exercise of the Pagan religion was unsuccessfully attempted to be effaced by the edicts of various emperors throughout the fourth century. It was not until near the close of the century that Theodosius, by laws of ferocious severity, succeeded in suppressing the public manifestations of' Paganism Even then we cannot doubt that in the country districts, out of the way of the imperial ministers and functionaries, the edicts were more often evaded than not. The very word, which came to denote the ancient religion – Paganism, or the belief of the rural populations – itself indicates the tenacity with which the peasant clung to the "creed outworn."

In looking back over a tract of time, which is long past, it is difficult to keep one's sense of proportion. It is hard to realise the change, economical and speculative, which was gradually creeping over the Roman world from the Antonines to Theodosius. We know that within this long period social life must have undergone a transformation far reaching and deep. Yet, viewed in our perspective, it seems comparatively slight. Too many links are wanting in the chain, too many threads in the woof to give us a true idea of the process. Everything seems foreshortened. The three centuries and a half which have elapsed since the last great epoch of organic transformation in society – that which saw the overthrow of the mediaeval civilisation, and which, like the preceding one, took the form primarily of a revolution in religious belief and observance – has been fertile in such vast changes that all other corresponding periods of change and transition seem to move imperceptibly in comparison. The impassable gulf which divides modern life externally, no less than in its habits of thought, from all previous ages, dwarfs and foreshortens the other great transitional periods of history. Progress, i.e., the content of time, has become immeasurably compressed; the development of a thousand years is now concentrated in a hundred, a hundred in ten, &c. The change from the second to the fifth century was, as far as the essentials of life were concerned, though great, yet not so great as the length of time would lead us to imagine at the first moment of reflection. A period of three or four centuries had still to be passed over before society had finally succeeded in definitively reconstituting itself on a positive basis in what we know as the middle ages. Thus, if the ancient world was long a-dying, no less long did its corpse remain unburied – still the ideal of glory and beauty to reflective men.

Notes

1. It should be observed that already in the first century the practice of burial had begun to supplant that of burning.

2. See Burkhard's Der Kaiser Constantin und seine Zeit.

3. Bohn's Library.

II

3. Liberalism vs. Socialism

A Lecture Delivered in the Conference-Room of the National Liberal Club

(November 1890)

What is the crucial distinction between Liberalism or Radicalism and Socialism? This is a question very often asked. That they are actually often opposed is not to be denied. But the general opinion seems to be that Liberalism, if its principles are thoroughly carried out, is not in any necessary conflict with Socialism. We propose to examine this position with special reference to the economic basis respectively of Liberalism and Socialism. The Liberal party has always claimed to be the party of progress, to be the exponent of the progressive lines of social and political development at a given epoch, and, as such, to be opposed to the party of reaction. This may be termed the negative side, of Liberal theory, and so long as it maintains this attitude as the party in the vanguard of progress, it must necessarily become identical with Socialism – i.e., from the standpoint of Socialists. But here comes the crux. If Liberalism becomes identified with Socialism, it surrenders bodily all that has hitherto formed the positive side of its theory, and, indeed, what has hitherto given it the reason of its being. It has up till now placed the freedom of the individual as the professed aim of all its measures, and as its basal principle. But does not Socialism also aim at the freedom of the individual? we shall be asked – assuredly. What, then, did and do Liberals (for the most part) understand by this freedom of the individual, or individual liberty, and why have they always made it such a strong point in their political faith? The answer is, they meant by individual liberty, first and foremost, the liberty of

70

private property as such, to be uncontrolled in its operations by aught else than the will of the individual possessing it. What was cared for was not so much the liberty of the individual as the liberty of private property. The liberty of the individual as such was secondary. It was as the possessor and controller of property that it was specially desired to assure his liberty. Indeed, in the extreme form of "Liberal" theory and practice, as embodied in modern legislation, the individual appears merely as the adjunct of property. Property is the substance the personality of its owner is the accident. And why was and is this? Because, we answer, the Liberal party represented the struggle of the middle-classes with expiring feudalism and absolute monarchy. It had to fight against the privileges of nobles and corporations, against institutions which hampered or prevented the free acquisition of wealth by individual effort, and the free application of that wealth when acquired. Its watchword was, therefore, individual liberty. The middle ages contained in its polity ideas of privilege and of corporate ownership which, after that polity had become effete, only hindered progress. Liberalism combated these effete mediaeval institutions on the line in which progress was moving – that of the freedom of the individual and his property. Thus far Liberalism was a progressive force.

Let us for a few moments trace the history of Liberalism, understanding the word in a wider sense than that of mere current party politics. Under the word Liberalism I include, for present purposes, the Protestant movement of the 16th century for freeing the individual from the control, spiritual and temporal, of the Catholic hierarchy; its descendant, the Puritan and parliamentarian movement of the 17th century, which culminated, after various vicissitudes, in the Whig party of the 18th century, which again subsequently became merged in the Liberal party of our own day. This great historical movement, extending over three centuries of the history of this country, from the middle ages downwards, must be viewed in its inter-connexion to be properly understood. In the course of the necessarily brief view we shall take of it, I shall endeavour to show that, while Liberalism (in the broader sense of the word here referred to) was at first true to its principle, and that it was really the champion of the rights and liberties of the individual, that in assuming that the chief of those rights consisted in the right to acquire and control property, it was really fighting the battle of the individual. For it was necessary that the trammels which bound the middle or capitalist classes to the feudal or landed classes should be destroyed, that the middle-classes should be emancipated, as the condition of all farther progress in the direction of individual liberty of any kind. But I shall hope to show, further, that, progress has now turned a corner, so to speak: that the removal of all hindrances to the acquirement of wealth other than what is based upon conscious fraud or open force: that the absolute right of the individual over the property he has acquittal or inherited – in short, that security and freedom in the tenure of private property is no longer synonymous with individual liberty, but often with its opposite; that individual liberty now demands the curtailment and the eventual extinction of the liberty of private property, and that Liberalism, in so far as if aims at maintaining the liberty of private property, is reactionary and false to the principle which it has always implicitly or explicitly maintained, of the right of each and every individual to a full and free development. In so far as Liberalism does this, in so far as it assumes as axiomatic a state of society based on unrestricted freedom of private property as far as possible under all circumstances, and proceeds to adjust social arrangements solely or primarily in the interests of the owners of private property – in so far, Liberalism and Socialism are death enemies. Liberalism has been negatively described by Sir Henry James as being alike opposed to Toryism and democracy, and this is, I think, no unfair description of Liberalism during this century. Liberalism has historically opposed itself alike to Toryism, landed interest, and democracy, working-class interest, whenever that interest appeared as a distinct political party. It has been the political creed of the middle-classes, which has used the war-shout of individual liberty as a means for the acquirement of individual property. The individual liberty now desired by the Socialist is the liberty of the individual as man, and no longer his liberty as mere property-holder.

The condition of England at the end of the middle ages, i.e., at the middle of the 16th century, was a remarkable one. The old system of laud tenure was breaking up, the villages and smaller towns were becoming depopulated, the sheep-farming system had absorbed much of the old tillage land; the land of the monasteries and trade-guilds was confiscated and had passed into private hands; the old peasantry were therefore driven on the soil and had become vagabonds; the new world-market – the extension of commercial relations, especially the importation of corn and the exportation of wool – had changed the conditions of production and distribution; the old guild system was breaking down in the towns; the country artificer was now everywhere a tradesman working for profit, but hampered by feudal laws and customs. Individual capitalists were struggling with the old city-corporations for the mastery, or establishing themselves in unchartered towns. The yeomanry or smaller landholders which had become an important, perhaps the most important, factor in English political and social life since the Wars of the Roses, were now established more firmly than ever, and with a growing influence. The desire to amass wealth, in the form of personal property, in contradistinction to the desire to command land and the labour of those upon it, now dominated men on it scale unknown before. To put the matter briefly, in England, the old dominant classes of the middle ages – clerks, barons, guildsmen – were dissolving and disintegrating, and new classes were growing up: in the country a, non-feudal, non-military class of small land-owners and tenant-farmers, many of whom were also artisan capitalists, distinct from the mediaeval knights and their socage tenants; and in the towns a class of independent capitalists, large and small, for whom the trammels of the mediaeval guild-system had become a hindrance and a nuisance To take one illustration only of this The number of apprentices and journeymen a member of the guild might employ in his workshop, the quality of the material he might use in his manufactures, the mode of conducting his business generally, were all regulated down to the minutest detail by the ordinances of the guild, to which the guildsman had strictly to conform. Now, the conditions of production anti distribution were outgrowing the rules of the guild which were made for much simpler and less extended operations. It was now obviously the interest of every man to produce as much as the rapidly extending markets demanded, and to employ as many men as suited him. In the middle ages, when the burgher class was imperfectly emancipated from the thraldom of noble and ecclesiastic, and where markets were extremely limited and extremely difficult of access, the guild, with the strict discipline it involved, was a necessity for the existence of the urban industrial community. Now these conditions were fast disappearing, it was no longer so, but it became the interest of every manufacturer and merchant to have a free hand to outbid his neighbour. What is said of the towns applies also (mutatis mutandis) to the country; the small yeoman, who was also an artisan, and traded on a limited scale, wanted free scope for acquiring all the wealth he could by his exertions, unharassed by feudal tolls and restrictions.

The interest of these new classes plainly lay in the direction of individualism, that is, of the severance of all the ties which bound a man to his village, to his lord, to his guild. All that stood in the way of the pursuit of wealth by the individual was obnoxious to the new classes. A new code of social ethics, as we may term them (as distinguished from theological ethics), grew up in accordance with these ideas. The shiftless class of proletarians which had formed alongside of the new middle-class or capitalists, on the suppression of the monasteries and the enclosure of the common lands, had necessarily turned to mendicancy. Now the new middle-classes found it to their interest to engage the free labour of those unfortunates at as little as possible, and not to let them subsist on the alms of the charitable. Accordingly the old mediaeval and Catholic idea that mendicancy was honourable yielded to the new middle-class and Protestant idea that mendicancy was disgraceful. This is interesting as the parent of the modern bourgeois notion of the stigma attaching to the receipt of poor-law relief. These new middle-classes were then the first individualists – the first Liberals opposed alike to the feudal noble and to the propertyless journeyman or vagabond. They ridiculed and affected to despise the propertied classes which were above them; they laughed at their literary embodiments – a Falstaff or a Don Quixote – but they and their henchmen were equally zealous in keeping down the propertyless classes that were below them – in suppressing a Kett's rebellion in England and a peasant's war in Germany. But nevertheless, as compared with to-day, the Liberal prototype of the 16th and 17th centuries was comparatively consistent. The propertyless class which has no control over land and the other means of production was, as yet, undeveloped and more or less transient. It was possible for the greater part of the population to earn a competency by their labour. The yeoman had his plot of land, the journeyman for the most part his tools and his skill as yet unsuperseded by the machine industry, so that the power lay with the vast majority of men of acquiring property by their own individual labour, over and above what was necessary for their immediate subsistence in tolerable comfort. Thus the individual citizen of this period might have been defined in the language of the logic-books as per se a wealth-producing animal. That wealth, produced in general, largely, if not entirely, by his own individual exertions, was not unnaturally held by him, the individualist, the Liberal, as of right belonging to him. He objected to being tied down by feudal exactions, he objected to the king having the right to levy contributions and taxes without his consent. In the ideal sphere the individualist principle was maintained. The new classes proclaimed the Protestant doctrine of individual salvation in theology as opposed to the old Catholic doctrine of salvation in virtue of belonging to a corporate body – the church.

These two sides of individualist faith have almost always gone hand in hand, and the salient point in the social ideal of the Liberal, whether in the shape of the Protestant yeoman, or burgher of the 16th century, the Puritan roundhead of the 17th, or the Whig, merchant, farmer, or squire of the 18th, or of the (in the narrow sense) liberal plutocrat and philanthropist of the 19th, has been, and is, implicitly or explicitly the freedom of the individual to acquire wealth in any manner he pleases – perhaps barring overt fraud or force – and to retain full possession and control of that wealth when acquired. Property held in severalty is and has been, in short, the groundwork of the Liberal creed in all its phases, inasmuch as the Liberal has always protested against the privileges of status and the institutions growing out of the mediaeval survivals of the early principle of property as held in common. The fact that Individual Liberty as thus formulated could ever be anything other than the only true individual liberty, never occurred to the Liberal individualist. Up till the end of last century, the economic conditions incident to the continued survival, to a very large extent, of handicraft-industries, and the fact that the population had not as yet begun to increase in any considerable degree, hid the real problem of the freedom of the individual. He still seemed the arbiter of his own fortune if only he were freed from oppressive laws. The only opponents of liberal individualism seemed privilege and rank and bad laws. What these were in the last century will be familiar to every reader of Adam Smith, Porter, or Thorold Rogiers. The law of parochial settlement which bound the labourer to his native village, the assessment of wages by the authorities, and other oppressive enactments and relics of old institutions served not only the upper, but the middle-classes with means for enriching themselves, the holders of property, at the expense of the working-classes of town and country alike. For it must not be supposed that having acquired his own individual liberty as a property-holder, the middle-class Whig was any more anxious than the landowning Tory to carry out his principles to the extent of emancipating the labourer from the oppressive customs and legislation against which he protested when it was his own interest to abolish it. For in the earlier phases of Liberalism there was no idea even of a logical and universal carrying out of its own doctrines of equality before the law and freedom of contract. Still it must be admitted that these principles lay in the conception of Liberalism, that the bourgeois having once invoked them for his own purposes against the aristocrat, could not go back upon them, that their realisation only awaited the economical development which would force him to concede and ultimately even to champion their universal application as the sheet-anchor of his system. The far-sighted Adam Smith saw this, and doubtless other Liberals of the last century saw it too. They saw it as the necessary deduction from their own principles, but they could not see beyond it. As I have before said, from their point of view it might have seemed the ultimate goal of reasonable progress. The handicraftsman could always earn a living, it appeared to them, if only he could have his freedom of locomotion and of making the best bargain he could for himself, to which was subsequently added freedom of combination, &c.

But a change now supervened on industry which put an entirely new face on things. In the last decades of the 18th and first decades of the 19th century, the machine industry began that great revolution in the production and distribution of wealth which is not even yet consummated. This revolution meant the destruction of the system of handicraft industry, i.e., of production by the personal skill of the workman and its replacement by mechanical processes. The handicraft system which had been modified in the workshop system, where a number of workmen were in dependent association, a system which obtained in many industries during the 17th and 18th centuries, had, of course, already considerably weakened the independence of the individual workman. But so much still depended on skill even in combined labour, and such a large field still remained for handicraft labour outside the workshops and in country districts, that the gradual transformation went on without causing any violent disruption of the previous conditions of labour. It was the introduction of machinery and the increased facilities of locomotion which revolutionised them, and, with them, the whole of modern life. In consequence of this there arose, as soon as the new factors had begun to operate to any considerable extent – a double politico-social movement that of the working-class dispossessed and disturbed as to their old means of livelihood, and that of the younger and (even from a middle-class point of view) more enlightened generation of bourgeois and Liberal politicians. Some of these doubtless still thought, in spite of the revolution going on before their eyes in industrial affairs, that all reasonable demands of the working-classes would be met by the abrogation of bad laws and a more extended suffrage. Others, more acute, saw that things were tending in a direction in which it would be the material interest of the middle-classes to take steps towards a more logical carrying-out of their own principles as implied in the word Liberalism. The first of these movements – the working-class movement – began with the Luddites and passed over into the Chartist movement. The middle-class Liberal, on the collapse of the Chartist movement, succeeded in hoodwinking the working-classes with the nostrums of free trade, extension of the suffrage, and the like, i.e., with movements mainly connected with the development of his doctrine of the liberty of the individual as the possessor and controller of property. But the two movements proceeded for a long while side by side. At the same time that that first blind outburst of the modern Proletariat against the modern Capitalist class, the so-called Luddite movement, and its successor the well-conceived and organised Chartist movement were going on, the middle-class Liberal was agitating for the

Reform Bill which was to give him the franchise on the strength of his property-qualification, and he was also beginning his agitation in favour of free-trade, and the removal of various other hindrances to the propertied individual increasing that property by commerce, or other recognised means. Liberalism was therefore now entering upon a new phase. The middle-class was beginning to see that its interest lay in the full carrying-out of its ground-principles, rather than as heretofore in their merely tentative and limited application. The working-man, like everyone else, must be freed from artificial restraints in the acquirement of wealth, must be allowed free liberty to make what contract he pleased; this was the claim, at least, of the more advanced section of the party. He must be made equal before the law. Now the working-man for a long time heeded the music of the Liberal syren. Chartism went to pieces. The new Liberalism carried all before it. Trades-unions even at length became respectable, patronised by members of parliament and lord mayors.

We come now to our own day; we see now what was at one time an advanced wing of the Liberal party become the main strength of that party. Every representative Liberal is now prepared to go the whole length in the direction of individual liberty as founded upon a property basis. He is prepared to grant the full liberty of every individual to acquire property and to control property. But he is seldom prepared to go beyond this. The primary fact with him is still not the liberty of the individual man, but his liberty as property-holder. Now as we have said, before the rise of the great machine industry, even as late as the last century, when work depended on skill and the individual workman still possessed his own tools, when in short a man could reckon upon making a tolerable livelihood at most times and in most places, the contradiction between individual liberty simpliciter and individual liberty secundam quid – that is, on the condition of possessing and controlling property – was not

79

developed as it is to-day. The two things seemed more or less coincident. Keeping up this tradition, middle-class Liberals, in carrying out the principles of their individualism, have studiously blinked the fact that the changed conditions of production and distribution which have enabled them, without danger to their own class-interests, to concede in form the benefit of those principles to the working-classes, have at the same time deprived those classes of any material advantage from them. Production and distribution now being an affair of plant machinery and organisation on a great scale, the workman is hopelessly at its mercy. The labourer may be as free as the air, so far as legal coercion is concerned, but the economical coercion of the private possession of the instruments of production and distribution presses upon him with an ever increasing force. It even affects the possessor of this property in many cases; he, too, although in a less onerous way, is often coerced by the economical conditions under which he holds his property.

Now the Socialist, in contradistinction to the Liberal, recognises to the full this contradiction between the two individualisms, the individualism which centres in personal property, and to which Socialism is opposed, and the individualism which presupposes the abolition of private property, at all events in the means of production, and which is identical with Socialism. He sees that the first is a purely abstract and formal individualism which sacrifices the real freedom of the individual to his merely nominal freedom. He finds that the workman is the slave of economic forces beyond his control, and that the way of real freedom for the individual, as for the society, lies in a revolution in economic condition which must involve the negation of the liberty of private property. When the essentially social functions of production and distribution cease to be regulated by the caprice and selfish interest of the propertied individual who holds the key to them, the time will then come, the Socialist sees, when individualism, in the sense of the possibility of the full and free development of the individual as such – of each and every individual, in contradistinction to that of the individual in so far as he belongs to a certain class or as he possesses property – will be realised for the first time in history. The word individualism has, however, almost invariably been used in the former sense, that, namely, of the freedom of private property, and has implied a condition of things in which every man has free hand to fight for himself without regard to his neighbour. This was the individualisms for which the so-called Manchester school, the backbone of English Liberalism, has fought. It could never, of course, be logically carried out without the dissolution of all social relations, but it has nevertheless been held up as an ideal to be striven after in so far as compatible with the exigencies of a social state and with the aspirations of the capitalistic classes. That production and distribution were social functions, and that to allow the individual to play fast and loose with them at his caprice was just as suicidal in the long run as allowing him to play fast and loose with human life on the highway, they could not and would not see. They restrained the individual liberty of the highwayman when, by means of his own property, to wit, his pistol, the latter fiercely offered the belated wanderer his money or his life, because they felt the conditions of the contract were unfair, and that the individualism was one-sided. They could not see that the manufacturer, in offering the propertyless labourer the free choice between his labour and his life, by virtue of his (the manufacturer's) property, the factory or the mill with its appurtenances, was also unfair, and the individualism equally one-sided. In truth, there is a good deal to be said for retaining the special word Individualism for the sham, abstract, one-sided individualism usually connected by the word, for the word itself implies a conflict between Individual and Society, and therefore is no longer applicable to a state of things in which there is no longer any conflict between the Individual and Society; for such a state is the outcome of Socialism, that is (so far as economics are concerned) of the corporate ownership and working of the land and other means necessary to the production and distribution of wealth. This is not said in any utopian sense, but in a simple, matter-of-fact one. To take an obvious case: let us suppose an individual is co-operating in the making of the communal or social bread. Since he, as well as the rest of the community, will suffer if the bread is bad, he being one of the consumers of that bad bread, and seeing that he can gain nothing in any other direction by putting scamped work or bad materials into the bread, his purely selfish interest is identical with that of the rest of the community in making the bread as good as possible. The same all round. It is the interest of the individual capitalist to make things as cheaply as possible – cheap materials and cheap work meaning bad materials and bad work. But the stimulus of self-interest to bad and dishonest production once removed, and you cease to have bad and dishonest production. By sheer force of circumstances the interest of the individual becomes identified with that of the society.

There is a great deal of talk by individualists about a "man's earnings," "the right of property of each man in that which he produces," etc. But what I ask, does each man produce of himself as an individual? Show me how much cotton any given factory operative has produced in the course of a year – I don't mean the amount of wages the capitalist has given him for the exploitation of his labour-power during that period but the actual product of his labour in the manufactured article. You could not do so, because his, like all modern labour, is associated: and the work of the individual producer is completely and indissolubly merged in that of the group (factory, mill) to which he belongs, which is again inseparable from that of the machinery employed in the process and from that of other groups. It is sometimes said liberty is inseparable from property, and I agree. But the individualism of private property has to-day landed us in a state of things in which the majority have no certain property at all, and therefore on the individualist's own showing the majority are deprived of liberty. Liberty, in any society, is inseparable from property. Good, but this does not say it is inseparable from private property. It does not say that it is not in antagonism to private property as we contend it is, in any case, where that private property is used for the social functions of production and distribution. No, liberty may be inseparable from property, but nowadays it is inseparable from the common holding of property by the community.

The outcome of Socialism is, then, a real individual liberty as opposed to a sham – a liberty for all individuals as opposed to a liberty for certain individuals only – in short, a human individualism as opposed to a class individualism. As for the nonsense talked about coercion under Socialism, does anyone suppose for an instant that Socialism implies any more coercion than what is absolutely necessitated by circumstances? This coercion you have under any state of society, and never more than in the present day when the economical laws of our anarchical, competitive, social state leave scarcely a single human being free to do as he lists. How many persons are there who can live just as they like, or do what they like with their time? How many can eat and drink what they like? How many can sleep as long as they like? There is coercion of circumstances dogging our steps at every turn and every hour of the day. The difference between the coercion of natural forces and of the economic conditions of a free competitive society and that of Socialism is that the one is a blind, unregulated, so far as we are concerned, a capricious power left to assert itself to the full over the unlucky individual; while the other is a consciously exercised and regulated coercion whose aim is, by the light of economic science, to minimise the former to the uttermost. The one means coercion untamed, the other coercion tamed. All Socialists look forward to the day when even the minimum of rationally regulated coercion involved in a Socialist society shall be no longer necessary. But, meanwhile, our choice is only between coercion at its maximum, dominating everything and everybody, as what I have spoken of as the coercion of circumstances – the coercion of the capitalist world – does, and coercion at its minimum, clothed and in its right mind and dominating as few departments of life as possible, as the coercion of the Socialist world would do. Here, then, we have this difference: Liberal individualism wants to perpetuate the unrestricted liberty of private property with the despotism which circumstances, economic and otherwise, exercise blindly and relentlessly upon every individual not possessed of private property, and often indirectly even upon those who are possessed of it. This is the basal principle of the middle-class movement of to-day. On the other hand, you have Socialism, which aims at getting rid of the despotic coercion imposed by existing conditions upon men, and substituting in its place a rationally conceived order of things, in which coercion of all kinds shall have been reduced to the minimum, and a real freedom obtained for all alike. This is the basal principle of the working-class movement of the present day. For the working-classes, even of this country, after having for more than a generation past hearkened to the voice of Liberal politicians, show unmistakable signs of awakening to a consciousness of their true interests – to sum up the question as between Individualism and Socialism.

The conflict of interest between individual and society is, as a constant phenomenon of human existence, but a growth of yesterday, if we compare its duration with that of the life of man on this planet. In primitive society the individual has no interests separate from that of the group – clan, tribe, or village – to which he belongs. Land and other property is held in common. He has not, as yet, awakened to a definite consciousness of himself as a self-contained whole. He cannot or does not think of himself except as the element of a larger whole – to wit, the group. There is as yet, therefore, no distinction of interest, either in fact or in sentiment, between the individual and the community. The distinction first asserts itself with the rise of civilisation, developing more and more into a formal antagonism as time goes on. Property held in common gets displaced by property held in severalty. This is the basis of political society with its centralised state, as opposed to kinship society with its limited group. The individual holding property acquires leisure and becomes aware of himself as a personality; he yearns with an ever-increasing yearning for the, as yet, forbidden fruit of complete individual autonomy, i.e., his complete formal independence of all the ties which had previously bound him to the community. The economic condition of the autonomy of the individual is, it must be borne in mind, property as held in severalty, in opposition to the primitive system of property as held in commons. I may remark here, of the two systems – the primitive one of property held in common and the later one of property held in severalty – that we refer to the predominating mode of property-holding. Absolute Communism and absolute Individualism in this, as in other respects, have probably never been realised in any society. Certain appurtenances of the individual, such as clothing, weapons, &c., have been tacitly recognised as accruing by customary right to the individual, even under the most complete and perfect form of primitive Communism. Similarly with our modern capitalistic society, which we may regard as, in most respects, the perfect historical expression of Individualism, in the common acceptation of the word. Here also there are, and always have been, certain things, such as public parks, museums, &c., which are, or are supposed to be, held for the common benefit. This is where, in my opinion, Mr. Sidney. Webb fails when he seeks to draw conclusions from the fact of the sporadic existence of public property in the present day as to the Socialistic tendencies of the modern bourgeois world. The real point of the distinction between Primitive Barbaric Society and Modern Civilised Society is that the first was based essentially on the commnon holding of property – the individual holding of property, when it existed, being purely accidental – while the second is based essentially on the private or individual holding of property, the common holding of property, where it exists, being similarly accidental to its main structure.

Now, individual autonomy (which must not be confounded necessarily with individual liberty, which is a much wider conception) is the expression of an opposition between individual and society, an opposition or contradiction which is very far-reaching, and which is the keystone to a whole hierarchy of similar though subordinate oppositions, whose development constitutes the subject-matter of the history of civilisation. To mention a few of these haphazard – in Economics, rich and poor, landed and landless, master and servant, noble and base-born, city and country; in Politics, governor and governed; in Metaphysics, soul and body, subject and object, thought and thing, God and World; in Ethics, sin and holiness, purity and impurity (as applied to the sexual relation); in Religion, sacred and profane, reverence and irreverence, world and Church, &c., &c. Now, in primitive tribal society, all these things were merely latent, implicitly and not explicitly present. What at first were undifferentiated and undeveloped functions of an organism in short, accidents of a substance – primitive society – on the dissolution of that society gradually acquired the character of independent, mutually opposing interests embodied in classes having severally these interests for their raison d'etre. Society (civilisation) meant henceforth no longer a coherent whole, but merely the aggregate of these interests as embodied in their respective classes. The simplicity and homogeneity of tribal society was such that it knew of only one opposition, that between the tribe or federation of tribes and the alien. The principle of contradiction in tribal society was external to that society itself. Under civilisation, while the old external contradiction tends to become abolished, contradiction has appeared in the very heart of the Social organism itself. Its salient expression is the contradiction of interest between individual and society, as expressed in the longing for individual autonomy; and its most salient embodiment is the modern Liberal individualist.

Modern Liberal individualism is thus, in a sense, the highest formulation of the principle of civilisation. The Liberal individualist is an extremely high product of civilisation. He is "Der Weisheit letzten Schluss" of the civilised world. But if, as we have said, progress for well-nigh four centuries has been making directly for individualism in the sense of the middle-class Liberal, and thus far Liberal individualism has been the expression of the progressive force of historical development, inasmuch as it has meant the liberation of the individual from the effete forms of tribal society which largely obtained throughout the middle ages in a modified guise, and of which the very trading guilds themselves were an offshoot – if this be true, it is none the less true that this work is now accomplished in all countries in the van of civilisation. Mediaevalism is broken down all round; the surviving relics of the social and political organisation of the elder world are either gone or fast going; the individual is emerging free and equal before the law, or as much so as he is ever likely to be in a class-society. The great thing which now oppresses area is, not the privilege of status, but the privilege of wealth. It is not the legal position into which a man is born that weighs him down, it is the contract he is compelled to make of his own free choice if you will excuse the bull). Progress therefore on the old lines of individual freedom before the law has plainly reached, or is fast reaching, an impasse beyond which it is impossible, and would be useless if it were possible, to go any further. Liberal individualism is therefore played out. Progress towards freedom, in short, has, as I said at the beginning of this lecture, turned a corner. Its old position has landed it in a contradiction, inasmuch as the attainment of the maximum of formal liberty has produced a maximum of real slavery. Free contract under a system of unrestricted individual property-holding has strangled liberty. We are to-day struggling with this fell contradiction. To suppress one of its terms is impossible. The resolution of the contradiction involved in the present, social, and economic situation, is, as you doubtless all know, according to Socialism, the socialisation of all the means and instruments necessary for the production and distribution of wealth on a huge scale with the other changes in politics and ethics which must necessarily accompany or follow this economical change.

In summing up let us view human development as a synthesis – as an articulated whole – we shall then see better the drift of the position I have sought to place before you here. Humanity grows up under the reign of a system of corporate or social interest in which the individual has no significance, except as the element of a social organism. This social organism is limited by conditions of kinship, real or supposed. The individual gradually attains to a self-consciousness which chafes against his subordination to the kinship society out of which he has grown. He at the same time emancipates himself from the bonds of this society by means of the institution of' private property and the centralised "state."

This is at once the condition of his autonomy, and his autonomy is the condition of the further development of the institution of private property. The two things are reciprocally bound up together. Endless anomalies result from the conflict of the two principles. Thus the head of the community, from being its father and the steward of its interests a primus inter pares, degenerates into the king or feudal lord. The old idea of leadership of equals gets mixed up with the new idea of individual property-holding, and the king acquires a right as of possession over the lives and property of what are now his subjects.

History shows us the idea of the autonomy of the individual forcing itself through these anomalies ever more to the front – again and again defeated – again and again asserting itself, each time more logically than the last, until, finally, in this nineteenth century, the right of every individual to autonomy has been conceded. But now when the victory is won – a victory necessary in the interests of progress, and without which Socialism would have been impossible – it is seen that individual autonomy, that is, individual liberty as conditioned by private property, is a failure, inasmuch as the institution of private capital is inconsistent with liberty in any other than a formal sense. The middle-classes as the embodiment (against the corrupt survivals of the elder world, the landed aristocracy) of the principle of individual autonomy are now themselves confronted with the proletariat, as the embodiment of liberty, social and individual. The freedom of the individual in and through the solidarity of the community becomes now the watchword of progress. Individual autonomy, or the liberty of private property – once the only conceivable form of liberty at all – implied the negation of the bonds arising directly or indirectly out of the crude homogeneous solidarity of tribal society; the liberty of the future implies the negation of this negation. Liberal individualism has opposed itself to the crudities and anachronisms of the old order and its survivals. Socialism opposes itself to the anachronisms of Liberal individualism, and as such represents a return to the communistic principle on which primitive society was based. It does so inasmuch as under Socialism society ceases to be a mere aggregate of classes and class interests, and becomes once more a connected system or whole. The functions of social life lose their character of independent entities subsisting for their own sake and. become once more merely functions – accidents of a substance, and not self existing substances. But it is a likeness in difference. The essential truth at the basis of primitive Communism will be preserved. The essential truth at the basis of modern Individualism will be preserved also. The solidarity, the associative principle of the one reappears in Socialism, but fused with the definiteness and the solicitude for liberty of the other in its best aspects. Modern Socialism embodies the truth of both principles, but purified from the crudities and limitations of those principles in their original form. What in them both, which was false and fleeting, dissolves. The goal to which human society from its first appearance has been unconsciously struggling, the synthesis of human solidarity and human freedom, will have been reached in Socialism. The first cycle of human development will be complete. The problems which have oppressed humanity, problems which have centred in the antagonism between individual and society, will have been conquered and for ever settled. That further developments may arise, new problems demand solution, further contradictions show themselves on another plane of the nature of which we can at present have no possible conception, is no concern of ours. Those evils with which we are affected will be gone for ever. What Socialists claim is, that the co-operative community which they are fighting for is the telos of human development to which history points. Civilisation having accomplished its world-historic mission, passes away into Socialism. Just as the principle of Individualism, though often defeated by privilege and rank, the survivals of the older principle, again and again re-asserted itself, each time with more emphasis than before, so now Socialists confidently look forward to the ultimate victory, in spite of all temporary disappointments, of the great principle of human solidarity. On which side in the struggle is liberty, in its true, its real, its concrete sense, can no longer be doubtful to any student of economy or history. To destroy the specious counterfeit, and in its destruction to realise the true liberty – to abolish the property-holder and free the man, such is the aim and such must be the outcome of the modern Socialist movement.

E. Belfort Bax

4. The Curse of Law

(August 1889)

Among the many curses the system of private or individual property-holding, which is the basis of what we call civilization has laid on mankind none is more conspicuous than "law." We here refer to civil law; criminal law which, properly speaking, arrives on the scene at a later stage in social development falls under a rather different criticism. The disputes between individuals having their origin in the private ownership of property afforded the opportunity for a class of parasites to arise who could for their own purposes exploit these disputes. The earliest form of legal decision in the earliest dawn of civilization, the decision of the Basileus, Rex or head of the tribe or gens can hardly be reckoned as belonging to the domain of law proper. It is not until these primitive social unities have been broken up, or at least their cohesion essentially weakened, that the reign of law and of the lawyer begins. Rome under the mythical kings knew no law. Homeric Greece knew no law. The legislator, the more or less mythical author of the legal code, is a familiar figure in early history. Thenceforward the curse of law has established itself. The written code may only have formulated the unwritten custom which had subsisted before, but this had reference to disputes between social groups, and not between individuals except in so far as they represented social groups. It was as the importance of the individual per se emerged that the written code arose and was applied to the disputes of private persons, and with this written code men appointed to administer it. Thus the class which preys on all other classes obtained possession of the field, and in certain periods of civilization has dominated society completely.

There was a fiction of the old legends, which stated the origin of law as follows:– Once upon a time (as the fairy-tale has it) two men were disputing on the highway about the ownership of some property, a third man coming up offered to arbitrate between them, they assent, and as remuneration for his trouble he receives a share of the property. Here, then, we have origin of the judge and his salary, the counsel and his fees, and the solicitor and his costs. Many persons may be inclined to wish that they had been one of the disputants in question with a six-shooter in their pockets; in which case they might have called their adversary aside, and only agreed to accept the decision of this primeval representative of jurisprudence on the secret mutual agreement thereupon to give the said worthy, as a reward for his trouble, not a portion of the spoil, but a couple of slugs each, impartially in the lower part of his body. This would have been less likely than the former procedure to have encouraged others to pursue the calling of meddler in other men's quarrels. But I need hardly say this pretty little myth is not exactly historical, but belongs to the a priori school of Rousseau's Social Contract and similar fictions of the last century, and that the administrator of justice was not at any period of his development to be got rid of in such an easy and effective manner as the above. In any case what concerns us here is not so much the origin of the man of law or his position in ancient or mediaeval times as his meaning and significance in the society of to-day.

Like every other profession or subordinate class, the legal class constitutes simply a privileged wing of the great privileged class of the modern world, the class which lives on the surplus value obtained by capital. The main trunk of the capitalistic classes finds it now more than ever necessary to the carrying on of its system that it should have disputes officially decided, and contracts enforced, &c. The importance of the class which is concerned in this confers upon it certain exceptional privileges. It constitutes itself into a "ring," ranging historically from the supreme judge to the ordinary attorney, a ring whose chief aim it is to promote the interests of the legal profession and openly pledged, by what is impudently termed professional etiquette, to stand in with each other, irrespective of inherent right or justice. Thus, after the conduct of Sir Richard Webster in the Pigott case, the legal members of the House of Commons refused to express their disapproval by voting with the minority, solely on the ground of this "professional courtesy." The position of advantage possessed by the legal class through its knowledge of the mass of chicanery under which the whole of the wealthy classes of the community, especially in this country, find it convenient to place themselves, enables them to assume the right to extort practically any terms they please for the most trifling act which they may perform for the layman whom they succeed in forcing to resort to them.[1] The legal profession from one end to the other thus forms a close corporation and is therefore a fitting pediment to the main edifice of middle-class society or modern civilisation. The capitalist fleeces the workman, the lawyer fleeces all round, the capitalist allowing the lawyer to fleece even himself, as he is thereby enabled to secure his hold not only of the workman, his natural prey, but of his brother-capitalist who is poorer than himself.

Were it not for the costs attending "law" the wealthy man would obtain no special advantage from it. The dominant class – the great capitalists – therefore sanction the fleecing practised by the lawyer and the courts even though they themselves may sometimes be affected by it, knowing that it furnishes them with a weapon with which to terrorise or, if need be, ruin their poorer fellow-citizens. Let thus much suffice (as Aristotle would say) for this aspect of law as embodied in our middle-class society.

The most important question connected with the present subject is the relation of law to morality. Throughout the historical period there has always been a covert opposition between the two things, which ever and anon has broken forth into open antagonism. "Law" and "honour" have always appeared at opposite poles. This is only natural, inasmuch as morality in its original intention implied a social relation. It was that power which bound men together in the fraternal bond, real or imagined, issuing from the notion of kinship on which early society reposed. As civilisation advanced this primitive morality was obscured by the new conceptions to which I have elsewhere given the name of the "introspective morality," which formed the Alpha and Omega of ethical sentiment in the relation of the individual soul to the divine being. But ever and anon the old instinct manifests itself, the original sense of the word was never completely lost. The bond of primitive society sprang out of the nature of the conditions of that society. If it cannot exactly be described as voluntary it was just as little coercive. Now "law" which has its raison d' etre not in any common tie between man and man but in the very opposite, to wit, in the assumption of the isolation of the individual, nay, of the enmity between man and man, rests definitely on the notion of forcible coercion of the individual and his interest. The old principle of ethics in its turn now assumes definitely the form of the voluntary regulation by the individual of his immediate egoistic impulses in favour of others, as opposed to the new principle of law which means his forcible coercion.

We meet with this distinction in places where we might not expect. For instance, in the Pauline epistles we find it taking the form of the antagonism between "law" and "grace": the principle of voluntariness or spontaneity from within is here opposed to the principle of forcible coercion from without. This, which is an abstract way of looking at the matter, since it only records one aspect of the antithesis, and which is used in the interests of the introspective morality, is none the less significant on that account. For this very antagonism between law and justice is susceptible of being carried out much more drastically than has ever been done hitherto. These two principles though they have existed side by side during the period of civilisation, have never really combined, but their essential incompatibility has not before been so flagrantly manifested as under the system of modern competitive commerce, which in its operations avowedly recognises no relation between man and man other than that of self-interest, and consequently in which the principle at the basis of coercive law is most fully realised. But as a matter of fact it has never been able to carry it out to its logical issue. It has been obliged to supplement it with a public opinion which exacts an adhesion to the rules of the commercial game, apart from law and on moral grounds, and stigmatises any departure from these rules as immoral and dishonourable. While on the one side it proclaims that business is business and scorns the introduction of sentiment into business operations; on the other it whiningly appeals to the sense of honour in order to supply any accidental defects in its own system of self-interest backed by coercion. The present writer was led to reflect on this subject some years ago in observing certain moral phenomena, as for instance, the readiness with which persons, whose honour was unimpeachable in private relations, did not hesitate to perpetrate a technical "fraud" on a Railway Company (and that this went on in spite of the assurances of the bourgeois press that it was quite as dishonourable to travel in a higher class to that for which you had paid your fare as to borrow money of a friend and not return it); also the difference universally recognised, implicitly or explicitly, between a debt of honour, which could not or would not be enforced legally, and a trade man's bill which could and would be so enforced.

Now these ethical phenomena seemed to me totally inexplicable on the conventional theory which confounds legal obligations with moral obligations. Such widespread instincts do not arise, in the general way, without a very good reason. The reason I pointed out some years ago in an article on Commerce and Conscience, as being that the true moral instincts of men pierce through the hollowness of the conventional sham, which seeks to obtain a double sanction for the enforcement of commercial, i.e., legal contracts. Pursuing the same line of argument, we have only to consider the results, let us say, of a consistent and all-round non-payment of obligations incurred in the course of business to see that the sole concern of this bourgeois honour and morality is not the welfare of mankind, or any other sublime principle, but merely the perpetuation of its own economical system.

The question here is one of debt. Now debts are of two kinds. There is the debt incurred to a friend, or mayhap, to a benevolent stranger, through his voluntary act, which arises out of a personal relation between you and him. Such a debt in all probability either cannot in the nature of things or will not, for personal and social reasons, be enforced by process of law. Such debts like all others which are based on personal trust and bear no legal sanction, are matters of honour and the man who shirks them is a mean scoundrel. So far we are all agreed. But there is another class of debt which does not arise out of any personal, relation but out of a purely economic or business relation. In commerce, the human being with whom transactions take place counts merely as an engine for the transference of money. Certain Gnostic sects used to teach that the oeon Christ passed through the body of the Virgin (as they expressed it) like water through a pipe. The man in a commercial transaction is in the position of the body of the Virgin. He is merely a conduit for the passage of the Christ of the commercial system, i.e., money. All that is asked of him is that his credit should be good, that is, that he should have money at his disposal, and that it should be possible, if necessary, to coerce him legally to disgorge this money. Here, then, I say, there is no question of moral obligation. The two parties to the transaction do not trust each other as men, brethren, or fellow citizens, but merely in so far as the one sees the way to coercing the other to complete his share of the transaction. Commerce is the game that is being played.

A friend of mine in a good way of business, but whose interests as a business man do not obscure his intellectual vision, very candidly recognises this fact and gives instructions to his foreman when about to county-court a defaulting customer, to assure the said customer that he has not the least personal feeling against him, that he does not regard him as a dishonourable man merely because he seeks to evade the payment of goods obtained in an ordinary commercial way, but that he fully acknowledges that while he as dealer naturally seeks to obtain as much as he can for his goods – to sell them as dearly as possible – his customer as naturally seeks to get goods as cheaply as possible; to buy in the cheapest market and sell in the dearest being the highest acknowledged principle of that commercial system which abhors sentimentality like nature of old abhorred a vacuum. Now obviously the cheapest way of obtaining goods is not to pay for them and if a buyer can avoid payment for the goods he obtains he has quite as much right to do so as the seller has to receive for them double or treble their value and call it profit. "We are playing a game," my friend would say to his defaulting customer, "at which we both seek to win, I hold the trump honours, law, in my hand; if by the aid of them I win – well; if in spite of them you win well also (though not so well for me.)" All is fair in love and war, and in competitive commerce, which is only war with a changed face. No one has a right to blame the tradesman for employing the natural weapon of commerce, coercive law, where we blame him is that when this fails he snivels morality and whines that his customer is a dishonourable man.[2] For heaven's sake let us free our minds of this cant and recognise that as things go there is no question of morality at stake, that the one in getting as much for the goods as possible, the other is getting the goods for nothing if possible, is each pursuing a line of conduct consistent with an individualistic basis of society, logically if not economically. We have said that the system of shop-keeping morality is designed, not with a view to human utility but to commercial utility – i.e., to the maintenance of the commercial system. This is easily seen if we consider the effects of a failure to pay one's tradesmen's bills.

This is a disgraceful and immoral act says the morality of the commercial system. If so, it ought surely to be demonstrable that some harm results, and not merely accidentally but necessarily results, to some individual or to the community at large from such a course of conduct. But what are the facts? Let us suppose Smith fails to pay his baker's bill; as a consequence his baker cannot meet his engagements with the flour merchant and has to go into liquidation paying something or other in the pound. The flour merchant not being able to meet his engagements with the corn-dealer has to do likewise, the corn-dealer, finding his relations with the factor considerably strained, is forced to undergo the same operation, the importer ditto; last of all the corn-grower also. The day-labourer is not affected, as the iron law of wages has already looked after him, and reduced his wages to as near the level of the means of subsistence as local circumstances will admit of. Now which of the above-mentioned persons is injured by Smith's proceeding. They all and severally, as we know, go on in business after their bankruptcy is settled as merrily as before. But let us suppose, what is, of course, impossible, that, by some means or other, legal coercion were universally suspended or evaded, that not merely Smith and a few of his intimate friends, but that all society took to not paying its tradesmen's bills, that in Kant's phraseology Smith's conduct came to be recognised "as a rule valid for all." What would happen then? Universal bankruptcy – the whole commercial world paying nothing in the pound. But in what respect does universal bankruptcy, which pays nothing in the pound, differ from universal solvency which pays twenty shillings in the pound. Immediately – in no respect whatever. The relative positions of persons is unchanged. "Being and non-being are the same." It is only in the qualitative differences which arise between these two extremes, within which the more concrete categories of commercialism work, that human beings are affected, There is just this ulterior difference, however, between the positive and the negative expression, that the positive, universal solvency (twenty shillings in the pound) is the ideal economic expression (albeit unattainable in reality) of a perfect commercial or individualist society, while the negative, universal bankruptcy (nothing in the pound, in short the abolition of private property) is the ideal expression of a Socialist commonwealth. So that on the Kantian maxim "so act that your conduct may be a rule valid for all," it is quite clear that Smith's action, if really followed by all, would, from an anti-commercial point of view, represent the highest morality. But this would not suit the commercial system, which adjusts its morality accordingly. (It may be observed, however, that since Smith's conduct neither would nor could be followed by all, while under certain circumstances it might through the friction it produced accidentally involve suffering to individuals, the most we can say for it is that it is morally indifferent under ordinary circumstances, and apart from any personal relation unenforcible by law which may subsist between the parties.)

The distinction between a legal debt and one which is only morally enforcible, and the feelings with which they are respectively regarded, may be illustrated by the case of the dispensation of hospitality by the modern hotel and mediaeval monastery respectively. Probably no traveller who has put up at that survival of the medieval institution, the Monastery in the St. Bernard Pass, has begrudged the voluntary contribution on leaving, or has given less than an equivalent for value received. But what man with human feelings in his breast has not at times felt a desire to bilk a hotel proprietor and evade the exaction of the often extortionate tax which the law permits him to levy on the unwary traveller.

Commerce, our individualistic method of production and distribution, is but a form of war – its weapon is law. "All is fair in love and war," we repeat. It is only the super-addition of a personal relation which gives a moral sanction to a commercial transaction. I have a friend who is in business, he gives me credit, not as an ordinary customer, but as a friend. I am morally bound to meet my obligations with him, and it is a mean and despicable thing if I do not do so. Moral obligation only obtains in the full sense, in short, where we know or believe that the "legal remedy" cannot or will not be resorted to. In a system that rests on coercive law honour has strictly no place. It is no use saying that law exists only for the man who is insusceptible of honour. It creates the man insusceptible of honour. Like the negro who was willing to accept the preaching and willing to accept the flogging, but resented the preaching and flogging too, so where you hold over a man the rod of law he naturally declines to listen to your appeals to his honour. If we are to be subject to coercive law let us be subject to it, if to morality or honour let it be so, but do not let us attempt to link in an unnatural wedlock the two principles, and appeal promiscuously first to one and then to the other.

Another point about "law," which is persistently disregarded by those who celebrate it as against "brute force," is that "law" is not like "conscience," something distinct from and in itself nobler than "brute force," but simply a hypocritical form of brute force. I say a hypocritical form of brute force because it pretends to be the exponent or embodiment of justice, and under this false pretence often enforces the perpetration of the grossest injustice. It is in the nature of things impossible to guarantee that legal decisions shall be in accordance with right. Social prejudice, personal antipathies, want of knowledge of those

100

peculiar circumstances of a case which cannot, or do not, always come out before a court, in short the proverbial frailties of human nature which pervert the judgment, render the pretence that law, under the most favourable circumstances, even remotely represents justice a fraud of the most impudent kind. Under the present system of Courts the ruinous swindling which accompanies law proceedings under the name of costs makes "law" or, as it is ironically termed, "justice," a mere engine of oppression. Many a man every day submits to the most flagrant extortion under the threat of "legal proceedings," because he knows that, however clear his case is, he is just as likely to lose it as to win it," and when the losing of it means a tenfold addition to the original fraudulent claim he naturally "grins and bears" the latter. As against this hypocritical sham which, with all the unction of solemn impartiality, forces a man to submit to being plundered, the unsophisticated "brute force" of the mediaeval robber-knight, by virtue of which without any "flam" of impartiality and justice, the traveller was despoiled cannot fail to strike an impartial thinker as noble and manly. Many persons imagine that if the civil courts did not exist and disputes were left in statu quo injustice would have to be submitted to without remedy. They forget that as things are, injustice is submitted to every day, rather than have recourse to the precious "remedy" civilisation provides, and that, generally speaking, the only effect of the "remedy" is to afford an engine of terrorism for the rich against the poor, for the strong against the weak. The fact is, that the legal method of settling disputes between individuals is a necessary bulwark of the system of individual property-holding, and of a class society on which civilisation reposes; it is simply a corollary of this system, and it is useless to seek any other justification for it.

We have alluded above to the essential uncertainty attending legal decisions, and their liability to error even under the most favourable conditions. This is a crushing argument against society in its corporate capacity undertaking any such function. When it does so, society knowingly makes itself responsible for unjust decisions, since, while it admittedly cannot guarantee the accordance of all decisions of the courts with justice, it still enforces all such decisions. It will be said, of course, that nothing is left undone to insure a fair decision, and that on the whole less injustice occurs under a judicial system than if the quarrels of individuals were allowed to take their course. Both these points, especially the latter, we should be disposed to vehemently dispute, but even granting them does not alter the case. Twenty acts of injustice for which society is not responsible do not weigh against one such act for which it is responsible. Society in using its collective power to enforce an unjust decision commits a crime. All are parties to that crime. If a man breaks a. contract he has made with me I have the simple remedy in my own hands not to enter into any further contracts with him and to denounce his conduct in the face of the world. Society is not responsible for the wrong done me. All that society is really concerned with in the matter is to see that the peace is not broken and to deal impartially with those who break the peace, no matter whether they are right or wrong in the particular question in dispute.

That ultimately civil law must disappear with the last vestiges of modern civilisation no Socialist will seriously dispute. But I still maintain, as before, that one of the first measures of a definitely Socialist administration should be the closing of all courts for the hearing of civil causes. Such a measure which would mean the definitive break on the juridical side with the old order is of too revolutionary a nature to proceed from any other than a revolutionary body, but given such a body, a new "Convention," or "Paris Commune, it could not consistently be refused. The saving in expenditure and the freeing of now useless hands for productive labour should alone commend it from an economical point of view. The question of the settlement of disputes between public bodies rests on rather a different basis. It might be necessary to retain an intercommunal or international tribunal for the adjudication of such disputes after the State had definitely renounced interference in contracts between individuals.

A point which naturally suggests itself is, in how far the foregoing observations as to the incompatibility of the ethical and legal sides of civilised life apply to criminal law. Directly of course they do not apply. The enforcement of a penalty on the commission of a crime has no direct analogy with the coercing of men in their ordinary civil relations. But even here, in the interests of a higher social morality, the minimisation of the sphere of law is in the highest degree desirable. The ideal condition of a community is that the remorse following the commission of a crime should be an adequate prevention of its commission. Now there can be no doubt that this sentiment of honour or conscience is weakened and a criminal class created precisely by the action of criminal law. Where a certain penalty is enacted as the price of a crime, there is a natural tendency to regard one as a set-off to the other and to make a calculation of the chance of detection, etc., etc., thus reducing the matter to a commercial question. The feeling that society provides it own remedy, pays itself, so to say, out of the criminal's skin, cannot but weaken the criminal's inner sense of his own duty – the spontaneous ought – towards society, and we may add indirectly not only of the criminal but of every member of society. The knowledge added to this that mistakes are sometimes made and cruel suffering inflicted upon innocent men by society in its own defence must still further tend to weaken the horror of crime as crime. The point alluded to above, that twenty acts of injustice for which society is not responsible are, morally speaking, of no importance compared to one for which it is responsible, applies with tenfold force to the case of criminal conviction. Better a hundred murders which the law does not father, than one execution of an innocent person which it does. In this respect barbaric custom, which does not recognise crime in the modern sense but only restitution for an injury done to the social group, has the immense advantage over civilised law. The above is, moreover, a crushing argument against brutal punishments, or, indeed, against any punishment more than mere preventive seclusion. It is not too much to say that a society that employs the gallows and the "cat" pretty much deserves all it gets at the hands of criminals. If the criminal, when he gets the chance of doing so with impunity, commits the crime for which the gallows or the lash is reserved, society has only itself to thank. In the natural course of things mistakes must arise, and innocent persons at times suffer those punishments. It is nothing but the most dastardly and abject cowardice, joined to brutality, which makes people run the risk for the sake as they believe of warding off danger from their own skins of becoming collectively guilty of such a hideous iniquity, Happily these punishments do not succeed in their object in most cases, and would still less, if every right-minded man did his duty when on a jury, and refused to convict for any offence to which (let us say) capital punishment or the lash was attached.

To sum up: Law we find as one of the first symptoms of civilisation. In barbaric society when at its zenith there is little or no conflict of interests between individuals, inasmuch as the individual is merged in the social group. When, with civilisation the individual gradually emerges from the group conflicts of interest between individuals arise – hence law, or the coercion of one individual on behalf of another by the State, now become the representative of private interests. The sentiment of honour now assuming the form of the conscious recognition of duty as opposed to self-interest grows up side by side with law but as time goes on is sure to be more and more antithetical to law. The one is mechanism, the other life. The notion that forcible coercion from without – law – and spontaneous action from within – honour morality are radically incompatible, constantly appears, a familiar illustration in literature being the antithesis of law and grace in the Pauline epistles, and in modern life the distinction between a legal debt and a debt of honour. Under the commercial system, the man of business seeks to combine as much sentiment with his system as will suit his purpose to help out the inevitable deficiencies of law and no more. To drive a hard bargain with a needy man, to impose on ignorance, and in short to obtain as much for goods as possible, by fair means or foul, is not usually deemed dishonourable on the part of the trader though it may thought wrong but for the needy man in his turn, in the teeth of law, to get the trader's goods for nothing – oh, that's naughty! My contention, on the contrary, is that, morality, honour, brotherly sentiment, "do as you would be done by," &c., presupposes a reciprocal personal or social relation, that where the relation is purely commercial and enforcible by law no such moral obligation obtains.

Again, law is only a masked form of brute force. In the same way that justice may be done by means of mere brute force of the robber-knight order, so it may be also by the brute force at the disposal of the tribunals, but injustice may likewise be effected by the same means. The important difference is that in the case of individual violence or injustice, society in its corporate capacity is not responsible, at least directly, whereas in that perpetrated in the name of law it is. Why should I be forced to participate as a member of society in the performance of an act which I regard as abominable infamy? That any consideration of mere immediate utility should outweigh this only shows the utterly low moral standpoint of the man of civilisation. Yet that it does out-weigh it we see every day in discussions on subjects of this kind. So long as a commercial system lasts a civil code will also obtain, which, under the sham of responsible justice compels Individuals to submit to its decisions, often in flagrant violation of justice.

That in the case of criminal law, mutalis mutandis, similar remark will apply indirectly, we have also pointed out. Probably few would deny the necessity for an indefinite period of a criminal code of some kind. The only thing we can do is to mitigate the inevitable evil,

1. by reducing the number of indictable actions to the minimum,

2. by hedging convictions round with every safeguard, and,

3. by reducing punishment as at present some of the Swiss cantons to mere preventative seclusion.

The foregoing observations, however, are primarily designed to explode certain common bourgeois fallacies as regards law rather than to further any immediately practical proposals. The writer is full aware of the historical significance of "law" and that no mere edict will suffice to root it out; although this does not say that such an edict should not have its place with other measures in the opening of a new order of things.

But the chief object of a discussion like the present is to induce people to abandon current prejudices which confound law and morality, which regard legal coercion as something intrinsically superior to coercion of another kind, etc., etc. That there exists a large number of persons who need clarification of their ideas on this subject, no one can doubt, who, having thought it out to some extent, has endeavoured to elicit the views of a generally intelligent and well-meaning friend thereupon.

Notes

1. One of the most impudent legalised forms of fraud is in connection with the taxation of the solicitor's bill, where it is only if the reduction of the bill exceeds a sixth of the total that he is compelled to pay the costs of taxation. The law in other words recognises his right to thieve, in so far as he can, up to the sixth.

2. The tremendous pull the law gives the tradesman, as such, over the consumer is proved by the fact that day after day claims are decided in favour of tradesmen on the sole evidence of the tradesman's Ledger. Any tradesman who likes to falsify his books can win any number of county-court actions, the onus of proof lying with the defendant that the alleged debt is not owing. After this to talk of honour in connection with a debt of this kind is rather naive.

5. A Socialists' Notes on Practical Ethics

(February 1891)

In a transitional period like the present, when the society of status has been superseded by the society of contract, the society of groups by the society of individuals in a commercial State, and when this society is itself becoming fast superannuated, when, like the mast of a ship on the horizon, the ideal of a new society based neither on status nor on contract, neither on the exclusiveness of the old Communism nor on the isolation of the new Individualism, is absorbing men's attention, an ideal which is as certain to be followed by realisation as the ship's mast on the horizon is to be followed by the ship's hull, it is but natural that our moral conceptions should be in a chaotic condition. We are between two moral systems, the Christian and bourgeois system of personal holiness and commercial morality, and the communist system of social morality. Hence, notions belonging to either of them are found intermingled in men's minds, and each man has to disentangle as best he can the principles which shall guide his daily life. Many of the canons of the current or bourgeois morality are justly felt to be no longer binding on those who reject the dominant system of society and its ideal. But with these maxims, which have significance solely in relation to the differentiae of an individualist-commercial or a introspective Christian society, are often confounded principles which underlie all moral relations whatever. Many persons who have given up the conventional bourgeois morality have not assimilated a socialist morality, and hence, have no morality at all. Their case is analogous to that of the savage who, under the instruction of the missionary, has learnt to despise the traditional and customary ethics of his tribe as "heathen," and having imperfectly understood the Christo-bourgeois mixture dealt out to him by the broad-cloth man of God, has developed into as ill-conditioned a scoundrel as it is easy to meet.

Now, for those who reject the moral standards of current society as such, it is of the utmost importance that they should come to an understanding; with themselves as to their true relation to this morality. The utter confusion of ideas on this point of many persons has been illustrated in the case of certain Anarchists who have not scrupled to commit and to defend any act of meanness or villainy on the ground of their emancipation from bourgeois morality. Now there are three elements in the current as in every concrete ethical system, in so far as it is ethical. There is the element which underlies all morality – the insufficiency and the abstractness of the individual per se, or as an end to himself, and the expression of this in the ought, of conscience, the impulse toward the realisation of self outside of self. But this element, although fundamental, is vague and abstract considered alone – having no definite purpose. It receives a determinate direction first in the definite categories of human relationship. Here we find certain general formula of conduct implicit, and more or less limited in their application in primitive society, and becoming more and more explicit and universalised in their application as civilisation advances. These general categories are the conceptions of Justice and Injustice, Meanness and Generosity, Fidelity and Treachery, etc. The mere indeterminate tendency is here negated, inasmuch as it acquires a definite direction, the concepts embodying it presenting themselves, not as the realisation of self, but as something imposed upon self – upon the individual – from outside. The categories named are the basal ground of all real or concrete morality. They resolve themselves, in fact, broadly speaking, into the propositions:

1. Every act necessarily involving cruelty is per se immoral.

2. No act not necessarily involving cruelty is per se immoral.

But the categories above mentioned, each and severally fall asunder into inner pairs of concepts which differ in different epochs within the historical period, and which are determined by the particular economic and other conditions of the epoch in question. Thus one age conceives justice and injustice in very different ways from another. The modern tradesmen would feel the regulations of the mediaeval guild an injustice. The medieval craftsmen feel it no injustice. Robin Hood, and those who sung of him, saw no injustice in plundering the wealthy merchant or ecclesiastic on the king's highway; nor, at a later date, did Sir John Fortescue, when he praised the English for being greater robbers than the French. Highway robbery was an act of war, and though illegal, was not immoral.[1] The appropriation of the wealth of another was to the average medieval mind only wrong under special conditions – i.e., when it involved meanness, such as the spoliation of the poor and the pilgrim. In the middle ages, indeed, the categories of justice and injustice always tended in the moral consciousness of the people to pass over into those of meanness and generosity, or treachery and fidelity. The notion of justice and injustice is more abstract and later in appealing to the mind. Then, again, in the case of meanness, barbaric notions of the sacredness of hospitality, the breach of which in all early societies is felt to be the most heinous of moral offences, as all early literatures show, and as may be seen to-day among many barbarous tribes, has disappeared totally from the ethical consciousness proper in most civilised societies. The categories of meanness and magnanimity in their primary sense have, in fact, lost much of their ethical force in a society of commercial individualism, though in their secondary sense even to-day they still form a not inconsiderable element in the ethics of modern life. Except in "business," which is an extra moral relation, being based on the autonomy of the individual, the taking of an unfair advantage – in other words, meanness – is still counted as a moral obliquity.

Fidelity and treachery, which embrace the categories honesty and dishonesty, truthfulness and lying – have also, undergone an immense change. In earlier ages the force of these lay in the breach of a personal or rather a social relation, now in the mere abstract act itself. To tell a lie to an enemy, or even merely to one outside the social group was not necessarily disgraceful any more than it was to rob the wealthy stranger on the king's highway. On the other hand, the betraying of hospitality, which is usually regarded as the most despicable of crimes in all early societies, would now be looked upon as legitimate under many circumstances. For example, some years ago the Italian Government sent some private detectives into Sicily with the view of capturing a band of peasants who had turned brigands, and were located in some mountain fastness in that island. The plan was for the detectives to personate peasant brigands and then to lead the real brigand band into a trap and hand them over to the authorities. The police-agents duly discovered their prey, who received them warmly, and with open arms, supposing them to be brother bandits, as they represented themselves. The best quarters in the ruined castle were allotted the guests, the best viands and wines, and a portion of the booty placed at their disposal. After a few days spent in a friendly and confidential intercourse, the detectives broached the object of their mission. They succeeded in luring the wretched brigands clown to the coast and on to a Government ship, under the pretence they were about to transport them to a hidden store of wealth on a neighbouring island. Once on board, the hospitable entertainers were of course immediately made prisoners, the chief pouring forth his contempt for the treacherous villains whom they had harboured. Yet, to the police-agents, this was all business. The brigands, who took the primitive view of the duties of hospitality, had offended against the law. It was the police-agents'

111

business to entrap them. But who shall say that these police-agents were on a higher moral level than the brigands?

What I may term the concrete and special (as opposed to general) moral principles of modern civilisation are based entirely on the private ownership of property. What divides the Socialist from the Radical is always and essentially this distinction of economic standpoint. I heard a prominent member of the Radical party, some months ago, say, he believed that in the future the man who had great wealth would regard it as a duty to devote that wealth to public purposes. This exactly hits off average radical ideals: improvement of the lot of the working-classes, accompanied by indefinite increase in the charity and public-spiritedness of the middle-classes – no conception of there being no man of wealth, of the extinction of the institution of private property, in other words, no notion of a classless society. So deeply engrained in us is this idea of class and of the holding of property in severalty, that we with very great difficulty conceive of any state substantially otherwise.

For this reason so few persons appear to realise how much of our ethics grow merely on the soil of severalty-property – that, for example, the whole of our sexual morality (as such), in so far as it has a rational, as opposed to a mystical, basis, is nothing but a "plant" to save the ratepayer's pockets by fixing the responsibility for the maintenance of children on the individuals responsible for the procreation of them, and that all "talk" of respectability, purity, and the like, is but the pale reflection of this central economic fact. But still it must not be forgotten that, as we are living under these economic conditions and not under socialistic conditions, any current standard of conduct must take them into account. It may deviate from the traditional and orthodox standard as much as one likes, provided that in doing so it does not ignore the facts which have given birth to that standard. It must make up its account with them in its own way, if it is not to come into conflict with those deeper moral categories which all morality at present conceivable involves. It must take them into account also in another, and to some extent an opposite, sense, if it is not to degenerate into the merely fatuous attempt to carry out Socialism in individual conduct in a society based on the opposite principle. Bearing these facts in mind, let us see how they work out in present-day social life. Now, a man may justly reject the dominant sexual morality; he may condemn the monogamic marriage-system which obtains to-day; he may claim the right of free union between men and women; he may contend he is perfectly at liberty to join himself, either temporarily or permanently, with one or more women; and that the mere legal form of marriage has no binding force. But this does not justify him in incurring responsibilities which he does not intend to fulfil. It does not justify him in seducing his friends' wives, or committing any other act of treachery. For the marriage relation, whether with or without the sanction of law, rests upon a reciprocal pledge of fidelity, which, although not absolutely binding, is certainly relatively so; that is, until full notice of the intention of withdrawal from it has been given by one or other of the parties to it. Similarly, under present social and economic conditions he is morally unjustified in taking advantage of friendship with a man for having, without his consent, a fleeting and secret liaison with a daughter or any other female relation who may be supposed to be under his protection, and whom he may have met in the course of social intercourse with him. Again, it is quite correctly regarded as a point of honour with a medical man or a teacher that the female patients or pupils with whom he conies in contact in a professional capacity, should be treated on the maxima reverentia principle. The same applies more or less to immaturity at all times and places. In short, the distinction of standpoint as to sexual morality may be briefly summed up thus: – For the Christo-bourgeois of the present clay, the sexual relation is per se immoral, and only becomes moral per accidens, i.e., under a special condition imposed from without. To the

113

consistent Socialist, the sexual relation is, on the contrary, per se morally indifferent (neither moral nor immoral) like any other bodily function, but it may easily become immoral per accidens, i.e., from the special circumstances under which it takes place, and whereby it acquires the character of an act of injustice or treachery, etc.

With the morality and non-morality of the relations of modern business-life I have dealt elsewhere. I have shown that the business relation per se is extra-moral and can only enter into the sphere of morality under certain special conditions. My relations with a man who is my friend, though they may be of a business character, are brought within the moral categories by virtue of that fact. I am not to him, nor he to me, any longer merely the X or the abstract buyer or seller of commodities, but this relation is inseparable from the other, and concrete one, that of friendship and social intercourse. Again, if a buyer or seller of wares befriends another, even without previous knowledge of him, that is, renounces for the nonce the law of the market, throws aside the weapon which, as a commercial man, he is entitled to use, the relation between them at once becomes moral. He, on whose behoof he has thrown aside the law of the market – business is business – is placed under the moral law as regards him who does so. His obligation is no longer merely an abstract, a legal, a commercial one, but a concrete, a personal, a human one. If any one alleges that on a consistent carrying out of this principle commercial transactions would become impossible, my only reply as a Socialist is – that is no concern of mine.

There is a good deal of confusion on the part of many persons respecting the true moral attitude of the middle-class Socialist, as to what is commonly known as "charity," also as regards the payment of wages, etc. One need scarcely at this time refute the commonplace bourgeois gibe that the capitalist, as soon as he professes Socialism, ought to strip himself of all his belongings merely for the sake of doing so. But it may, perhaps, be said he ought to spend all his wealth on the party as such. Now, there might be something in this, if it could be proved that it was advisable for the "party" to be taught to rely on windfalls from individual members. It is not to be denied that there are circumstances under which it may be the duty of an individual, or, at least, extremely commendable in him, to sacrifice his wealth for the cause. Such cases have occurred over and over again in Russia, and might easily occur elsewhere. But the fact remains that, in the ordinary way, nothing tends so to demoralise a sect, party, or organisation, as the acquirement by it of wealth without exertion, or the accustoming of it to expect supplies from more or less accidental sources. When a party once gets wealthy in this way, it becomes a centre of attraction for every worthless person and hypocrite; even men who at starting were genuine get corrupted, and quarrels arise among them over the emoluments to be obtained. When a cause has to rely upon resources of this kind it has little or no real vitality. Either it is dead in itself, or the time is not ripe for it. And though in the latter case a little factitious booming of the kind referred to may be good, yet this can very easily be overdone. Socialism, like every other great movement, has made headway, not through the lavishness of individual benefactors, but through the energy of the masses themselves, through their conviction of its necessity for themselves, and through the enthusiasm which has led each to contribute his quota to the cause of party-organisation and propaganda. Wherever there has been a systematically subsidised Socialist party it has been pro tanto a failure. Where it succeeds it is by the mites of the masses and not by the cheques of the classes. Certainly, a middle-class man may be legitimately expected to contribute a substantial sum, according to his means, on a special emergency, but in systematically subsidising the movement, experience has proved he is injuring rather than benefiting the cause he has at heart.

In matters of private "charity," as it is termed, there is no special principle to guide the Socialist, as such, any more than any other person. The desire to relieve the present suffering of individuals, when it comes under our notice, is natural and laudable, but the how, the when, the how-much, must be left to the feelings of every individual in his private capacity. This commendable sentiment does not, unfortunately, by any means invariably co-exist with a readiness to sacrifice class-advantages for the sake of a higher and a better social system. The charitable man in private life is often the most truculent reactionary in politics. There is, however, one aspect of the charity question which does sometimes nearly affect the middle-class man, who is also a Socialist. Such a one may possibly be an employer of labour in some shape or other. There is a certain market-rate of value of the labour he employs which may happen to be a low one. Now, there is no doubt that the giving of wages above the market-rate of labour, above what the labourer himself demands for his labour, is, in a competitive society whose basis is the market, exactly equivalent to charity. In saying this, I, of course, exclude the attempt actively to force down the rate of wages or to hold it down when it is rising, which entirely alters the case. But assuming, let us say, that in an unskilled, unorganised branch of labour, the labourer offers himself for a certain wage, is the employer, I ask, morally bound (I leave inclination on one side) to exercise charity in his particular instance by giving him more than such market-value of his labour? Let us hear both sides in the form of a dialogue!

X. How can you, who call yourself a Socialist, give the miserable wages you do?

Y. I give the wage which is admitted by the conditions of the market. I have never beaten down wages; but were I to give more my business would cease to be remunerative. Besides, in conducting business I decline to mix up charity with it. If I were to give more, that surplus would be a matter of charity, and as much a question for me as an individual to decide for myself as any other question of private charity, as, for instance, whether I give alms to a particular beggar at a particular street corner or not. Let the workmen in my branch of industry organise and demand a higher rate of wages, and it will, of course, be my duty to bow to the decisions of such a representative organisation.

X. Then you take advantage of the fact that these workmen happen to be unorganised in order to sweat them?

Y. That sounds plausibly ugly, certainly; but do not you, my friend, do not we all 'take advantage,' as you express it, of the system we have the misfortune to live under? Does not everyone who goes into business at all, or who invests money, be it only in a savings' bank, 'take advantage' of the system – does not everyone who lives under the system and who is above the worst-paid class of workmen 'take advantage,' in a sense, of those below him? And would it benefit anybody or any cause that he should not do so? What you, like a good many other people, confound, is the 'taking advantage' of a system already existent by the individual who lives under it, and the exacerbation by him as an individual of the evils of that system for his own selfish benefit.

X. But tell me in what way are you better than Livesey, Norwood or any sweater?

Y. Precisely in that I recognise the sacredness of the demand by an organised body of workers for higher wages or shorter hours, as indicating the sign of a change (little though it may be), a change that I, as a Socialist, should hail with joy, even though it meant the destruction of my business. Not to do so, let alone to attempt actively to resist it, would be placing my own personal interests above the common cause of the workers.

X. But you ought not surely under any circumstances to pay less wages than what are requisite for a decent subsistence?

Y. Unfortunately, the standard of living, even among the working-classes, is very varied, and the normal standard is, therefore, difficult to fix; besides, the modern industrial mechanism is so complex that even if a really tolerable standard were fixed, the individual capitalist could not, as things go, maintain it and continue his business.

X. Then let him stop business.

Y. Well said; but this would only mean the throwing of a number of workmen upon the streets, and the possible reduction of the small capitalist himself to the position of a proletarian.

X. Be it so then. Better let the unemployed workman starve than encourage him to accept too low wages.

Y. But absolute starvation would surely be worse than even the low wages which competition compels me to pay. The workman would surely lose rather than gain by my throwing him on the street by closing my business. It is quite a different thing when, with a definite end in view, he chooses of his own accord and with an organisation backing him to come out on strike.

X. But you must accustom him to the idea of not working for too low wages.

Y. Does he require then to be taught this? Does he work for the low wages because he likes it, and not rather because he must? Will the effect of my refusing to employ him at the market rate, and since I cannot afford to pay him a higher one, refusing to employ him at all – will the effect of this, I ask, be any other than to drive him on to the next man in the trade to accept the same, or, if possible, a still lower wage? In giving him the wages at which he and his fellows are compelled to offer themselves, I am not exacerbating the system, I am not taking advantage of any special circumstances in which this particular workman is placed; I am not forcing down wages or preventing them from rising. My paying my workmen over and above the market rate, as an individual capitalist, will not raise the general rate nor prevent them having to accept that rate when they leave me.

X. I repeat, after all that you may say, you have no right, as a Socialist, to employ men at wages which are below the lowest possible rate at which they can obtain decent food, etc. You ought to draw the line, at the very least, at the minimum union wage, that is the lowest wage which is admitted by any union, and recognise this as the lowest you have a right to give in any industry at any time.

Y. Now you give me a definite proposition which is worth thinking about and to which I promise to give my best attention.

I leave these arguments to the consideration of the reader's conscientious judgment.

We should always bear in mind that the bourgeois morality regards names more than things; the rose is not as sweet by any other name, in fact when it bears any other name than the one middle-class respectability has assigned to it, it is despised and rejected of respectable men. The stock exchange is a reputable institution. Staking money in stocks on the chance of a rise is business ("that blessed word"), and a perfectly legitimate occupation. Not so, staking money on the turf, at roulette, at baccarat, etc. This is gambling, the pursuit of frivolous, foolish and sinful young men. Then again, with marriage. Advertising is a disreputable form of obtaining a wife, at least in this country. But the London season, with its balls and garden-parties, in which the previously unknown young woman is introduced by her parent or guardian to the previously unknown young man, is a perfectly natural and praiseworthy institution. Why on earth a man with other things to do should have to put on a glazed white plaster over his chest, and wear a ridiculous black coat cut away behind in a positively indelicate manner, and talk platitudes for the sake of meeting a previously unknown member of the opposite sex with a view to matrimony, when, assuming he is as yet undetermined in his sexual inclinations, he might as commodiously compass his object by advertisement, seems at first sight beyond comprehension The real explanation is that the bourgeois, while wishing to maintain the present marriage-system, based on property-qualification, and on commercial considerations, wishes also to keep up the sham of its being based solely on idyllic emotion, and hence objects to its being carried on under the outward forms of commerce. The latter shocks his susceptibilities. Although the legally enforced marriage of modern society, is, in its nature, as much a commercial contract as any other, it seeks to hide this under certain conventional, social forms. Yet again, slavery is repugnant to the modern middle-class mind, or it is pretended that it is so (partly because it interferes with capitalistic enterprise in Africa and elsewhere), but in spite of the repugnance, real or feigned, of the modern man to slavery under that name, and when it takes the form of "status," he finds nothing objectionable in it at all in the guise of a sham "free contract." The compulsory subjection of the will of one man to that of another, which is the essence of slavery, acquires quite a different moral character when it is not called slavery, but wage-labour. So it is through all departments of life. Essentially, the same act which is condemned under one name is approved or tolerated under another, especially where the external conditions of it are slightly changed.

Let the Socialist lose no opportunity of exposing and showing his contempt for these frauds of the current morality!

The ethical issues opened up by an adoption of the Socialistic attitude in current society are various. We have indicated a few of them. But there are plenty of others which will occur to the reader. For example, there are law's made expressly to obviate evils for which the constitution of present society is responsible – which laws in the clumsy attempt to suppress the manifestations of a system, while maintaining the system itself, often come into collision with our deepest feelings. A noteworthy instance of this is the law which makes the concealment of a felony penal. Our natural and unsophisticated moral sense proclaims that the duties of kinship, or friendship, require us to protect the relation or friend to the best of our power even from the consequences of a crime, so long as this social relation has not been definitely broken off. Now, the commission of a crime may be a valid reason for breaking a friendship, and thus relieving ourselves of all further obligation, but it can never justify the betrayal of a friend to the vengeance of the law in the first instance. The feeling which revolts against the surrender of a person with whom we have been on terms of friendship or intimacy to his destruction, which is a survival of the solidarity of the primitive social group (whence came in later times the practice of compurgation), is a much more sacred thing, and its preservation of vastly greater importance to humanity than aiding the police-mechanism of the modern state to punish crimes for the existence of which it is itself largely responsible. This is to me perfectly plain. But a more difficult case arises when the act of a person, hitherto a friend, is of more serious import than most mere common law offences – as, for instance, if he were to turn political police spy. Now, the interest of the Socialist party requires under certain circumstances that such should be killed. Here, of course, there can be no doubt as to the duty of repudiating all further connection with such a man, but the question arises, should we, in this instance, be justified in rescuing him from his admittedly deserved fate? Perhaps even here any possible future harm he might do to that party with whom we are working would be less than that arising from the shock to the moral consciousness which an act savouring of treachery would produce – even though the treachery were done to a traitor.

Then to take another point. Supposing that in Russia or elsewhere, a sudden and urgent demand for material resources for party purposes arose, and that much hung upon its being immediately satisfied. Supposing again, that, as a last resort, a female member of the party were without any hypocritical pretence to sell her body to raise the money. Would not this be a commendable act? Given the elimination of the mystical theory of the sexual relation, and I should say yes. Prostitution for private gain is morally repellent. But the same outward act done for a cause transcending individual interest loses its character of prostitution, and acquires a new content; the form of mercenary love would hide the reality of disinterested devotion to a cause and love of humanity.

I may conclude with an exhortation to search all things ethical as the indispensable condition of really and truly holding fast that which is good.

E. Belfort Bax

Notes

1. Within living memory the Italian brigand has prayed to the Virgin for success in his expeditions.

6. The Economical Basis of History

(January 1891)

Socialists often talk of the economic basis and interpretation of history without always further explaining their meaning. This I propose to do in a few words in this article. The economic interpretation of history rests on a well-known, simple and obvious law of human nature, if I may be allowed to employ that often much-abused term. There are probably few of my readers who, if they had had nothing to eat all day, would prefer a lecture to a supper, were it offered them; nay, who would not prefer the supper to the finest theatrical spectacle imaginable, let them be never so fond of theatrical spectacles. The reason of this is that our human nature presupposes our animal nature, and that this animal nature must and will be dealt with before all else. So long as we are hungry, thirsty, cold, etc., the one object of our interest is food, drink, clothing, shelter, etc. These things are the one visible object of our desires; we conceive ourselves happy if we have them. We see, we wish for, nothing beyond them. Any organic or animal discomfort, be it a positive pain, like toothache, or a negative pain (a want), like hunger, makes us feel that its removal would be the consummation of all bliss. Balzac narrates a story in his Contes drolatiques, of a trick played by King Louis XI of France upon his courtiers, by which he prevented them, under circumstances of urgency, from fulfilling a natural function of the body. "Oh," said the archbishop to his neighbour, the master of the horse, "what pleasure in life is equal to," etc. Now, this story of Balzac's puts in an absurd form a very important truth, no less than the truth upon which the economic basis of social development rests – that the satisfaction of material, animal, wants takes precedence of all else in human affairs. The absence or threatened absence of the material conditions of existence obscures the desire of all else. The attainment or security of these becomes the one visible goal of energy. Instead of being the foundation they become the zenith of human aspiration.

On the other hand, when the means of comfortable living are there and secured, these material conditions of existence assume their normal function as the means and not the end of life. Just the same as the want of the necessaries of life obscures the desire of all else, so the fear of that possible want, when not actually present, also affords a like stimulus, a like indifference to all else than to the removal of the possibility of want. If we have enough food to-day, but feel that to-morrow we may possibly have to go without, the chief end of life still seems to us the assurance of a sufficiency. In short, wherever the consciousness of physical, bodily, material want, as present or as imminent, possesses us, we can see nothing before us but the removal of this want or the danger of it. The sight of superior advantages in another class also acts in the same way; the non-enjoyment of them is felt as a want to be relieved; everything, the whole object of life centres in the obtainment of the coveted position. Now, the endeavour after these things may either be confined to the individual who seeks to free himself from material discomfort and win for himself comfort – in short, to desert his class – and whose end in life is limited to this; or it may become a class instinct, a class endeavour, in which the whole class is engaged, and in which every member of a class feels his solidarity with his class, so that he is prepared to sink his individual interests in those of his class as a whole. We see the first illustrated to-day the commonplace man of the world, be he working-man or middle-class man, and the second, in the great working-class movements, and above all, in modern Socialism. The only aim of the former man is to place himself and his immediate family in a comfortable position. The aim of the latter is to conquer economic freedom for his class, inasmuch as he sees that there is no certainty for himself, and still less for his descendants, so long as his class remains in economic subjection. It is this latter form of unselfish selfishness, of egoistic disinterestedness, which is alone the lever of historical progress. We saw it exhibited yesterday in the emancipation of the middle-classes from feudal trammels, we see it to-day in the struggle of the fourth estate with Capitalism. What in the individual is at best merely low and sordid, though often excusable and natural, becomes purified and ennobled when the individual negates himself an individual in his class, always provided that class has human equality as its ultimate aim.

We see, therefore, that for economics to be the motive-power of progress, presupposes, to put the matter shortly,

1. a class in a position in which it is either deprived of the average necessaries and comforts of life possessed by another class, or in which its enjoyment of these is precarious;

2. a consciousness in the former class of this deprivation, i.e., a consciousness of its own inferiority and precarious success;

3. a belief in the possibility of its attaining the coveted comfort, leisure, or security by class-action.

These, I say, are the conditions for the economic movement to make itself felt in history. They are conditions under which, when present in a class forming the majority, or even a considerable minority in the State, they most make themselves felt. I do not say that they are always distinctly formulated; the class-consciousness spoken of, the consciousness of insecurity of social position, or of positive discomfort or want, may be, and often has been, rather instinctive than definite. But be it vague or clear, its removal constitutes the highest conceivable goal, political and social, for the members of that disinherited body. It is almost a truism, nowadays, that throughout history, classes have existed, and there is no period throughout history in which the foregoing conditions have not prevailed more or less. But I maintain that in precise ratio to the degree of their prevalence, has the course of history depended on the question of the production and distribution of wealth, in short, on economics. People used to trace all historical phenomena back to speculative or literary causes. How erroneous this view is is obvious when we consider that a man in want of food is actuated, not by the religious belief he may happen to hold, but by the necessities of obtaining food, which necessities may very likely modify his religious belief, while his mere religious belief is not at all likely to modify his economic necessities. Religious belief, superstition, or whatever we may like to call it, on the contrary, bends at once before the material exigencies of life. This was illustrated a few years ago in Scotland, when the chief article of the Presbyterian creed, the duty of not performing any useful or agreeable act on Sunday, was violated under the pressing danger of the loss of a harvest and consequent starvation, and when thrifty highland men and women were to be seen garnering in the sheaves of corn on the Sabbath. The pulpits indignantly fumed against the impious act, but still it went on in different districts for three or four Sundays in succession. The highlanders may respect the Sabbath, but they respect the inexorable laws of self-preservation even more.

The most striking instances of the way in which class-antagonisms and economic pressure become the direct causes even of religious change in society, are discoverable in the final dissolution of mediaeval and the foundation of modern society, in the period, that is, known as the Reformation. These causes are also conspicuous in the first of those great crises which denoted the overthrow of the ancient world and the establishment of Christianity. To take the latter case first. The cities of the Roman Empire exhibited a restless crowd of proletarians, emancipated slaves, whom it did not pay their masters to keep, of landless and moneyless freemen – the bulk of industry being still carried on by slaves for the consumption of their owners, such free skilled manufacture as there was being rigorously "protected" by the collegia or guilds, which had the monopoly of handicrafts and trade. The economical history of the time of Constantine and that immediately preceding is sufficiently obscure, but we can see that by that time affairs were in extremis. The great, peasant and proletarian revolt in Gaul, early in the reign of Diocletian; the laws of maximum and minimum which followed in 296 and which covered all the necessaries of life; possibly also the last great persecution of the Christians – all these things point to a period of great economical pressure. Then again the wealthy provincials were continually harassed by the dread of ruin. Under the name of Decuriones they formed a kind of local senate and were responsible to the fiscal administrator of the emperor for all deficits in the revenue supposed to come from their district. The Church at this time exercised the function of a general insurance society. It was a mine of riches which it distributed to those who had paid the premiums of "faith" and baptism. Its wealth was already enormous and attracted numbers, and its aim was to absorb wealth by any means within its power. Monasticism was advancing with rapid strides, and the ecclesiastical organisation was already a refuge for thousands who were otherwise dependent on the precarious support of patrons or the public donations. A tremendous impulse was given by the official establishment of Christianity under Constantine; the profession of the Christian faith became increasingly a means of livelihood. But the most significant thing of all in this connexion is the struggle between Paganism and Christianity which went on during the fourth century and which resulted in the final overthrow of Paganism. It must be remembered that Christianity throughout the fourth century was almost entirely confined to the town populations. In the total population of the empire the Christians were a minority.

Now what was the cause of the savage attacks on the pagan cults which took place during the fourth century? I answer with the late Mr. King of Cambridge; it was the desire of the ecclesiastics, in conjunction with the shiftless populations of the towns, to obtain possession of the enormous treasures locked up in the temples. That there was genuine fanaticism in the Vandalic destruction which took place, I would not deny, but there is to my mind just as little doubt that the direct economic reason was in most cases the leading one. The Christians of the fourth century were a noisy minority of the total population of the empire, and the overthrow of Paganism was accomplished like all other great revolutions in history by this active and energetic minority. The celebrated edict of Theodosius was the official expression of what had been going on for over fifty years. Precisely the same thing took place in the revolution which gave the death-blow to the mediaeval system and which also assumed the form of a change of belief. Then also the new middle class and the town-populations generally wished to enrich itself with the spoils of the monasteries. The Protestants up to the reign of Elizabeth, at least, were a noisy handful. The confiscation of the monasteries went on simultaneously with the expropriation of the people from the land, by enclosures and the formation of large sheep-walks, and by the transformation of industry, which gave rise on the one hand to the new proletariat, and on the other to the new employer class, together with the other great changes which destroyed or jeopardised the previous means of existence of large sections of the population. These classes found themselves, without any conscious determination on their part, forced into a reformative or revolutionary attitude, alike in politics and religion.[1] Their great enemy they saw in the old system of society with its trammels or free contract, its local imposts, its independent jurisdictions, its ecclesiastical organisation, and the hundred other evils which crushed them down or prevented them from rising.

129

The above are instances given very briefly of cases where the economic movement is obviously the dominant and leading one, and they might be multiplied a hundredfold. But it is a mistake, as I take it, to regard the economic side of things as in all periods of history equally determinant. For the material conditions of existence, the modes of the production and distribution of wealth to become the leading factor in determining the course of human affairs, it is, as we have already intimated, necessary that the whole community, or a considerable portion of it, should be vaguely or definitely conscious of the fact that its means of maintenance in average comfort are threatened if not already compromised. Now this has been the case more or less throughout history, that is, throughout the period we term civilisation, which has always been based on the individual holding of property and on the existence of propertied classes over against propertiless classes in some form or shape. But the economic element has not been equally operative throughout history. During periods of quiescence the dominant classes whose means of existence has been assured have not been subject to it, and certain forms of progress have taken place independently of it. For we must never forget the great fact that, although economics are the basis of human existence, they are the basis merely and not the complete whole – that we have to do with a synthesis, human society comprising various elements. As I have just said, though throughout the historical period the economical side of things has operated more powerfully than any other single influence, yet its operation has not been uniform. There have been periods when it has been counterbalanced by the concurrent action of other influences not deducible from it. It may contract so as to appear comparatively insignificant as an active force, just as it may expand so as to dwarf all other factors. For example, there is much in the history of the first two centuries of the Christian era which cannot be directly referred to economical causes. Fiscal exigencies will account for a good deal, but they will not account for all the speculative or all the political changes which form part of its history. Again, it would be difficult to deduce the rise of the Saracen power from the special conditions of Arabian society in the seventh century, or the Crusades from the conditions of the mediaeval manor of the eleventh century. In both these cases we obviously have to do directly with speculative causes. If we look into these periods we shall find, I think, that the means of existence on the lines of the current organisation of society, of the majority, or of a considerable minority of society, was not immediately threatened and that the dominant classes did not feel their position endangered. In the case of the Europe of the eleventh and twelfth centuries, for instance, though all living was rough enough, no classes were directly threatened by the then existing organisation of society as they were three or four centuries later. The Arabia of Mahomet's time, again, was in a barbaric and semi-barbaric state, in which classes either did not exist at all in an economic sense, or were only just beginning to show themselves, while we have no reason to suppose that there was any greater pressure of food supply, etc., on the Arabian tribe of the seventh than of any preceding century. We are here clearly concerned with movements having their roots in the ideological or religious aspect of human nature which came to the fore now that the economic side of affairs fell into the background. We see the same in the case of privileged classes who feel their position tolerably secure. There are certain human interests whose development cannot be interpreted economically, that is, referred to any large extent to economical conditions. The higher aspects of intellectual development usually come under this heading, the reason being that philosophic speculation, scientific research in its earlier phases, and certain, forms of art are developed within a wealthy and leisured class, i.e., within a class for whose consciousness economic conditions are at zero.

Economic conditions are a potent factor the first stage of poetry, the epos, which takes its rise in the popular consciousness at a time that class antagonisms are beginning. Again,

131

architecture is an art which, owing to its subordination to utilitarian purposes, is also powerfully affected its development by economic conditions. The same with all the decorative arts. Philosophic speculation, on the other band, which is never popular, and which does not arise except, as already remarked, within a class economically safe and sound, has no positive connexion with the prevailing modes of the production and distribution of wealth, – and, in fact, cannot in most cases even indirectly be deduced therefrom. The metaphysic of Plato and Aristotle has no assignable basis in the material conditions of Greek life. On the other hand, economic conditions may react on the results of speculative thought, may prepare the way for their acceptance by the popular mind, as also the media which shall interpret them. The great historical instance of this is the popular acceptance of the introspective morality – the morality of the individual and of personal holiness. This, which was in the first instance merely a speculative aspiration of isolated thinkers, fell upon a soil favourably prepared by the economical conditions accompanying the consolidation of the Roman supremacy, and rapidly spread, in the form of the Christian religion, among the vast free proletarian and slave population of the empire. But even here it may be doubted whether the political movement, the destruction of the ancient, independent city life, and the consequent breaking down of the old barriers and of the interests with which these barriers were connected, did not as much contribute to the spread of Christianity, and the other systems embodying the new speculative and ethical principles, as the one before mentioned. It was the latter, certainly, rather than the former, which must be regarded as the predisposing influence amongst the possessing classes. An economic interpretation of human, evolution presupposes in an advanced society an inequality of economic condition, the existence of classes, or, in other words, the private holding of property. Thus it is that throughout the historical period the economic movement has been a leading one, most commonly the leading one. But if this has been the case throughout history, what of the pre-historic period in which the highest social development was the tribal society of kinship with its economic basis of primitive communism? What of the society of the future with a socialist betwixt its economic basis of collectivist production for social uses? Has the economic basis been, and will it be the lever or motive power of progress in these cases? To take the former instance first. Owing to the undeveloped state of early man's resources over nature, tribal communistic societies are always liable to economic pressure from without, that is, from natural causes. Famine, drought, disease, are in such societies particularly fatal in character. They are always exposed moreover to attacks from without from other societies, and may be forced by stress of economic circumstances to make such attacks themselves. Hence, warfare is generally the most important and honourable avocation, and personal prowess the highest virtue of such societies. But in the internal development of such a society economics does not occupy the constant predominance as an active motive power that it does in civilised societies.

For example, the origin of the wealth and influence of priesthoods, in so far as this is to be found in pre-historic times, is not traceable to any economic condition, but rather to the speculative condition of the early human mind. It is true, fear of evil consequences, economic and other, for the society, induced special attention to be sometimes paid to the world of conscious and willing beings with which primitive man felt himself surrounded, and in whose hands he believed his destinies to be. But this did not originate the belief in these agencies. It was only one of the many circumstances in which the aid of the gods was invoked. Ancestor-worship, which in primitive and all early forms of society plays such an important part, is certainly not to any appreciable extent influenced by questions of mere material exigency. In primitive society the general aim may be defined as the maintenance, continuance and glory of the kinship organisation. In this stage the special goal aimed at is either not consciously present at all, or only vaguely so. The economic factor in the evolution of tribal society is only a leading one under special circumstances imposed from without. A sudden failure of food supply, or the pressure of other tribes, determines migrations, wars, etc. But, apart from this, under favourable circumstances, there is no reason to suppose that, within the tribe or kinship – society itself, the economic factor, per se, is more operative than any other.

The real point to be remembered is that we have to deal with a concrete synthesis – "social life" – and that all the elements which go to make this synthesis are organically dependent on each other. The basis is, of course, the production and distribution of the necessaries of material welfare: but this is an element, merely of a synthesis, and not the synthesis itself. In a primitive communistic society the several departments of human interests are as yet latent or implicit, and it is, therefore, no such easy matter to assign definite limits to each, as it is in a highly developed and differentiated society, where the domestic, economical, political, speculative, religious and artistic spheres are clearly distinguishable and even separable in function. Every social net in all early tribal society of equals partakes at once, more or less, of all these characters. Thus every public assembly of the tribe, in itself primarily a political act, involves, not as a mere accessory appendage, but as part of its essential character, sacrifices and other religious ceremonies, processions, music and dancing, the presence of the image of the tribal god, often feasting and other domestic functions, divination, astrological pronouncements (the early representation of applied science), while matters relating to the economical arrangements or position of the tribe may at the same time be decided. Now all these timings are so undifferentiated in primitive social life that it is difficult to say which is predominant. Under favourable natural conditions the economical movement will probably not be the decisive one. It is conceivable that a purely speculative belief might be the occasion of very important results. For example, it was presumably the quasi-religious veneration attached to the elders of the society, connected as it was with ancestor-worship, which gradually undermined the primitive forms of the gens and tribe and gave rise to the patriarchal family and the earlier phases of monarchy. It could scarcely have been on any other than superstitious grounds that the assumption of wealth and power by individuals was tolerated. The old modes of production may have proved unsuitable as the society expanded; the plunder taken in war, the capture of slaves, etc., may all have contributed to the accumulation of property in private hands; but without the religious element it could hardly have acquired the sanction of custom, since it was manifestly opposed altogether to the traditions and interests of the majority of a tribal society. But whatever element it is which is the immediate cause of change, the other elements which go to make up the synthesis are, so to speak, dragged along with it. The specific change denotes or is the sign of the advent of a stage in the organic development of the society. There is no such thing as a fundamental economic change without a corresponding political, social and religious, and even artistic change. And so it was in the change from primitive communistic society to civilisation. Every phase of social life underwent modification in a corresponding manner. The religious side of things was, as usual, the most conservative, and undoubtedly hindered to some extent the course of the political and economic revolution. This is especially noticeable in the religious conservatism of the old gentile forms.

When once the revolution which instituted civilisation, with its individual of private holding of property, was fully accomplished and fixed in law and custom, the methods of the production and distribution of wealth, in other words, the economic movement, became and continued in varying degrees throughout history the dominant factor in social evolution. As we have before remarked, this must of necessity be so whenever the economic equilibrium of society is disturbed. The private holding of property involves the existence of classes, of a class possessing property and the power which property brings when held in exclusive possession, and a non-possessing class who are dependent for bare living upon the former, at whose mercy they are therefore placed. Henceforward, in precise ratio to the development of the civilisation, to the concentration of property in the hands of individuals, is the importance of economic condition as the measure of progress. The ethical movement which is directly traceable to economics, is also noteworthy. With the indirect connexion of the new individualist ethics which ultimately gained the ascendancy over the earlier social ethics and the corresponding economic development, we are not here concerned. I have dealt with this at some length elsewhere. But there is one point which may be mentioned as illustrating the aspect of the question now under discussion. It is the notion of asceticism. The satisfaction of material exigencies is the conditio sine qua non of all the "higher" human activities. Now asceticism is, at least from one point of view, a recognition of this fact in an inverted form. The ascetic finds the material conditions of civilisation incompatible for most men with high aspirations. Instinctively feeling, therefore, the impossibility of finding a foothold in the quicksand of civilised life, in the sense of a satisfaction by social means of material needs, he seeks this footing in the arbitrary suppression of those needs by the individual. He preaches, and sometimes practises, the "simplification of life." This soon becomes his chief aim. He does not stop to inquire the use of all this simplification. In what sense the man who succeeds in making himself more uncomfortable than his fellows is better than they, never seems to occur to him as a subject of inquiry – at least, in the case of your Count Tolstois and other cultured modern ascetic preachers who claim to represent rational principles. This notion of suppression rather than satisfaction as forming the starting-point of a higher life, which has drawn its foul trail through the historical period, will assuredly pass away with the economic disabilities under which the major part of mankind have laboured during that period, and which are accountable for the "fox-and-the-grapes" like spirit to which it is due.

In primitive communistic society then, to return again to our more immediate subject, the economical movement only made itself apparent as the motive-power of social development owing to the interposition of external causes – resulting partly from the limited command possessed by early man over the forces of nature, and partly by the limitations of tribal society itself, which gave rise to continual hostilities with neighbouring societies. Throughout civilisation, on the other hand, it has been the dominant motive-power in most periods, though in varying degrees, for the simple reason that its prominence has resulted from a cause not merely external and casual, but one inherent in the internal structure of civilisation which is based on Individualism, and on the consequent existence of a propertied and therefore powerful, and a propertiless and therefore powerless class – the existence of these two opposing classes having implied the continually recurrent want or threatened want of the necessaries or average comforts of life by vast sections of the population, thereby raising the mere material conditions of life to the rank of the telos or end-purpose of all human endeavour. Hence the phenomena of avarice, and the attachment to money as money – i.e., as the symbol of security for the means of life – which permeates all civilised society. But now, how about the future?

The degree in which material conditions have influenced progress has been, as we have seen, ceteris paribus, in direct ratio to that concentration of the wealth of the community in private hands by which the livelihood of the majority is rendered precarious. In the present day this has reached a point at which the production and distribution of wealth is not merely the central point of human interest as it has often been before in history, but in which it has absorbed all other interests into itself. Other departments of human activity have become the more appendages – mere rudimentary offshoots – of this one. The one reality of the nineteenth century is the scramble for wealth; politics, literature, science, religion, art, are, apart from money-getting, mere lifeless wraiths. The necessities of modern life bind men like Ixion to the wheel of production and distribution. The mere economic machinery enslaves us to-day in a manner which it has never before done throughout history. To-day, therefore, the economic factor in evolution has acquired an unequalled importance, being, in fact, very generally, the only one worth serious consideration. But "when night is darkest dawn is nearest." The absolute despotism of economic interests and economic processes reduces life itself to an impossibility for some, to an absurdity for all. The moment the majority of men, the class immediately affected by it, become conscious of this, its end is at hand. The contradiction, whereby the means of living usurp the place of the end of life once fully manifest, must resolve itself, and there is only one way in which it can resolve itself. Whereas now the will of man is unconsciously determined by economic processes and economic interests, then economic processes and economic interests will be consciously determined by the will of man. For, it must be admitted, we are already in a fair way of conquering the powers of nature to the service of man, while in the society of the future, inasmuch as we believe it to be international in its character and organisation, war will have ceased. The causes, therefore, why economic conditions influenced the development of pre-historic society will no longer obtain. On the other hand, the internal organisation of society under collectivism implies essentially the abolition of classes, and of the private property-holding on which civilised society is based. The causes, therefore, of the ascendancy of economic condition in the historical period will also no longer obtain. But this pre-supposes a communistic organisation of society – an organisation for all, by all. Here, for the first time, will Human Evolution have once for all subordinated its material conditions, and subordinated them, not after the manner of the ascetic by the suppression of the desire for them, but rather by its satisfaction. Men will cease to think unduly of their appetites when the means of healthy satisfaction is within reach of all, when they are not, as now, debarred from it by social conditions. Here, for the first time, will the economical interest definitely cease to be the determining power of Human progress. The material conditions of life may be luxurious, or may be simple, according to the needs and tastes of the new generation of men; but in a world where the resources of nature, as developed by modern applied science, will be used and indefinitely further developed for the common advantage and not for the exclusive benefit of individuals and classes, where production will be regulated, expanded and contracted, from year to year, as common necessity may dictate, and, therefore, where "thrift" will have become an extinct virtue – in such a world it is manifest that economic developments will follow and not lead the desires and aspirations of men, and will no longer dictate the consequent modifications and re-adjustments which social life will from time to time undergo.

E. Belfort Bax

Notes

1. I do not dwell on this period, as it has been often dealt with by Socialist writers. For England, Hyndman's book may be consulted; for Germany, Engel's Bauernkrieg, and for a general view of the situation Kautsky's Thomas More, especially the Introduction up to p.120.

7. Individual Rights Under Socialism

(21 March 1891)

The opinion is commonly held by those whose views of things are determined by the sound of words, or who are given to swallowing ideas without sufficiently masticating them, that the chief aim of Socialism is the annihilation of the freedom of the individual, and that ergo anything that tends in this direction is pro tanto Socialistic, and anything that tends in the opposite direction pro tanto Individualistic, in the sense of anti-socialistic. Because Individualism is the name given to the existing system of unrestricted competition, i.e., to the unlimited control by the individual of the productive and distributive powers of the community, in short, to the attempt of the individual to make himself absolute, or asserting himself at the cost of other individuals and of society as a whole, therefore these sapient critics think the essence of Socialism to consist in the limitation of individual freedom: We need scarcely say that the notion that the maximum of Socialism corresponds to the minimum of individual liberty is as preposterous a travesty of any great principle as ever entered the perversest head of man. Socialism demands the greatest possible liberty (or licence if you will) of the individual, limited only by the condition of its not infringing on the principle of equality of liberty. When the exercise of individual liberty is at the cost of equality of liberty; when it is a liberty of some at the expense of all, then necessarily Socialism steps in and proclaims the curtailment of such liberty. But in this case and only in this case, is Socialism not identical with the greatest possible extension of individual liberty. For example the liberty of the individual to waste the resources of society by producing wealth in the most costly rather than the least costly manner, such as occupying land as flower gardens which ought to be used as cornfields, thereby entailing unnecessary labour on the rest, is not a liberty which would commend itself to a Social-Democratic community. But on the other hand, in all really "self-regarding actions," that is, actions which directly affect the individual performing them alone, complete freedom is of the very essence of Socialism. And yet one hears sometimes when a protest is made by a Socialist against some absurd and tyrannical infringement of individual liberty on the part of the existing law, some callow idiot tender the observation, "But surely that's Anarchism not Socialism". The reply is simple. Unless Anarchism had contained some element of truth in common with Socialism it would never have deceived so many good-hearted but weak-headed Socialists as it has done.

As a matter of fact, it contains two such elements, each of which it exaggerates and divorces from its connection, erecting it into a sacred principle independent of all else, thereby falsifying what would be true if viewed in subordination to other aspects of the Socialist problem. The first element of truth in Anarchism is that force is as justifiable in the hands of revolution as of reaction, and that there is no inherent reason why it should not be successfully resorted to. This Anarchism travesties in its cultus of violence as the sole justifiable method of working for revolutionary ends.

The Second element of truth is that above stated, to wit, the freedom of the individual, the non-coercion of the individual by the society, as an end to be striven for. This it certainly is, since the play of individual initiative is an essential of the development of society considered as an organic whole. But the Anarchist travestie this truth by converting it into the holy dogma of the abstract freedom of the individual at all times and in all cases. I say the abstract freedom, for rather than coerce the individual for what was obviously the collective good, his own included, by limiting him in the commission of the most

141

preposterous acts of folly and destruction of both, the consistent Anarchist says: Perish society, perish individual.

In the desperate attempt to preserve the abstract and formal appearance of freedom the aforesaid Anarchist is willing to fling its reality to the winds. For the reality of human freedom, if not of human existence, implies organisation based on social evolution, which is incompatible with the idea of absolute formal autonomy of the individual. The only sphere in which the individual can claim absolute right to autonomy is in that of those self-regarding actions which do not in any direct manner touch his relation to social life and in these Socialism demands it as completely as any Individualist can desire. But in things as constituting the fibre of social existence, as such, such as economics, that is, the production, distribution and regulation of the necessaries of life, such autonomy must inevitably mean the re-enslavement of man under the forces of nature.

Yet, though the only place in which Socialism demands the absolute freedom of the individual is in "self-regarding" actions, the tendency of Socialism is toward the minimisation of coercion in every department, especially of direct coercion. For example, take the foolish talk often heard about the difficulty in a non-competitive society of dealing with the idle, dissolute, &c. The problem correctly stated is, what not to do with them. i.e. how best to cut them off pro hac vice from the advantages and even necessities of the social life against which they are sinning while leaving their formal freedom as individuals unimpaired. An organised system akin to boycotting might possibly serve the purpose. The aforesaid persons, assuming them to be physically and mentally capable, deliberately refuse to contribute their share to maintain the organised freedom which the commonwealth of the Social Democracy has developed. That commonwealth, while refusing them the benefits of that freedom, magnanimously allows them to retain their individual autonomy and see what they can make of it. Thus, the bestowal of the individual autonomy so much desiderated by a certain school of Anarchists might come to be the punishment allotted to that class of persons who bulk so large in the estimation of certain objectors to Socialism.

It is exceedingly probable that, once Social Democracy has gained the upper hand over Civil Society, the punishment of crime (in so far, and so long as it exists) will be on similar lines. The increasing revulsion of the human conscience, as a rule, not only against brutal punishments but against any punishment at all which is of a positive nature – i.e., to the proceeding by which the modem State in cold blood, and as a purely mechanical act, seizes the criminal and torments him – has its significance. It is one of those symptoms -which denote the awakening consciousness of the better sort, even of middle-class persons, to the fact that modern civilisation is not the best possible thing in the best possible of worlds. The difference between the view taken of crime by the middle-class individualist and his State and by Socialism, is significant of the relative position of the two. To the individualist, naturally, the particular criminal as such, is solely and entirely responsible for the crime he commits. On him, therefore, he wreaks all his vengeance. To the Socialist, on the contrary, for every crime committed, the State, or the society in which it is committed, is as much or more responsible than the individual. When you have once ceased to regard the individual as an isolated and abstract moral entity your ferocity against the criminal is gone. As a mere matter of self-defence you may reserve to yourself the right to slay the ruffian if he attempts to practice upon you, or to assist any other victim to that end, if you are in the way. But the truly bestial ferocity with which the average bourgeois gloats over the cold-blooded torture or butchery of the garrotter or murderer by the law becomes merely repulsive. The humane and refined law of England in the

143

platitude of its wisdom naturally takes the opposite view. It forbids a man under pain of penal servitude from preventing himself being garrotted or murdered, but zealously flogs or hangs the garrotter or murderer after the event.

Now, the idea of society being itself partly responsible – partly itself guilty in the matter of crime – naturally, on reflection, and after the heat of momentary indignation at a particular crime is over, engenders a consideration for the criminal which forbids us to regard him as the executive of the modern State does, as a being without rights and without human qualities. We feel that society deserves to pay the penalty if it produces criminals, and that, though the criminal may conceivably be utterly depraved, yet that he is not necessarily so, and in most cases is more sinned against than sinning. Hence the feeling of cowardice and injustice as attached to the calculated infliction of suffering upon the individual criminal by the collective forces of society. This feeling, as I said before, I take to be the foreshadowing of a treatment of crime by which the penalty will be deduced from the crime as a natural consequence of it, rather than assume the form of a deliberate act of vengeance. In short, the part played by society then will be negative rather than positive. Violence is always double-edged in its moral aspect. Granted the right of society to inflict suffering, in itself wanton and useless, upon the criminal and call. it punishment, one can hardly refuse to admit the right of the criminal to similarly revenge himself upon the society or, at least, the executors of its vengeance. By wanton and useless suffering I mean such as merely hurts the criminal without repairing the effects of the crime or otherwise benefiting the community. Thus to imprison a man with crank and plank-bed for a theft (we assume, of course, private property as surviving) is a wanton act of vengeance. But to compel him to labour till he has restored by his labour fourfold its value, only placing him under such restraint the while (if at all) as is absolutely necessary to prevent him shirking his task would be a punishment logically

144

deducible from the crime itself. Given the right of society to torture the criminal uselessly and you at once get into a vicious circle of acts of vengeance and revengeance from which there is no logical escape. The mind naturally revolts against the infliction of wanton suffering.

The negative attitude of society referred to above, which was the principle on which crime was dealt with the early world, will probably be the form which, mutatis mutandis, its treatment will take in that later world on the threshold of which we are, but which we have not yet entered. The community in this case would withdraw its protection from the criminal citizen, and while leaving his formal liberty unimpaired, would deprive him by social ostracism, if not of his bread and salt as in ancient Rome, of all but the barest necessities of life, together possibly with the right of invoking its protection under certain circumstances – in fact, place him under a ban. There are cases in which the penalty might be very directly deduced from the crime. Thus, supposing the case of a man who whenever he got drunk was in the habit of committing acts of violence. Nothing further would be required than to notify to such a person that the fact of drunkenness placed him at once outside the protection of society, which would mean that in addition to the other dangers he incurred when in such a condition – falling down wells, area steps, steep places into the sea, etc – there would be yet another one in that any assault upon him under these circumstances would be regarded prima facie justified. This, I take it, would be quite as effectual a means of preventing him from getting drunk as the dread of a possible three month's "hard." The mechanical police-system of the modern civilised State and its penal codes must inevitably be superseded by a psychological method which refuses to ignore the special motives and characteristics of individuals.

Law, the positive coercion of the individual by the State, will become modified into the coercion of a public opinion which leaves the offender so severely alone that he dreads the alone-leaving even more than the actual violence of the jail. The development of penal methods along lines somewhat similar to the foregoing, viz., the reversion to the principle of a negative rather than a positive action on the part of the social body as against the individual offender – must, I think, without doubt be a sequel of the change from Civilised to Socialistic conditions.

I may conclude by repeating what was said at starting, that one of the aims of Socialism is the minimisation of the positive and mechanical coercion by society of the individual in all departments at human life. Although the individual in a Social-Democratic Commonwealth will in reality be knit together with that commonwealth inconceivably closer than he now is with the modern State, yet it will be the imperceptible union of one element in an organism with the whole, rather than the connexion of a cogwheel in a complex machine with its main apparatus. Direct, mechanical, coercion arose with Individualism, and will fall with it. Where society exists merely as an aggregate of self-centered units having, separate and opposed interests, there mechanical coercion is a necessity. As soon as you have a real as opposed to this pseudo-society, so soon mechanical coercion gives way before organic union – the antagonism between individual and social interests, from being an integral element in the constitution of things Human, is reduced to a mere sporadic accident, or altogether disappears.

8. Marriage[1]

From Outlooks from the New Standpoint, pp.151-160.

There are few points on which the advanced Radical and the Socialist are more completely in accord than in their theoretical hostility to the modern legal monogamic marriage. The majority of them hold it, even at the present time, and in the existing state of society, to be an evil. Yet strange to say, they, most of them, contract these legalised monogamic unions, the excuse being the stigma on offspring and other inconveniences which are attendant upon the adoption of any other course. That there is considerable inconvenience in any other course cannot be denied. It cannot be denied that this is largely because persons who profess to be otherwise emancipated, and who ought to know better, pander to the current view by adopting an ostracising attitude toward at least the female side of the illicit equation. They defend their action in rather lame fashion, urging the convenience of current society and the general desirability on grounds of expediency of legal forms. It is to these persons that I chiefly address myself.

Let us see, first, to what historical period the strict monogamic marriage primarily belongs. Needless to say, it begins with civilisation; but in the early stages of civilisation the tie is loose; polygamy is indeed the rule here and monogamy the exception. Throughout ancient civilisation the right of concubinage and of hetarism even in the Graeco-Roman civilisation, often also the duty of showing sexual hospitality (the offering of the wife or daughter) to guests. Christianity tried to impose strict monogamy on the world, but signally failed. Whether monogamy was originally any more than a counsel of

147

perfection in the Christian scheme may be doubted, especially in view of the Pauline injunction that a bishop was to be "the husband of one wife," which looks very much its if the "humble" Christian was at that time very often the husband of more than one wife, like the ordinary free subject of the empire, who, as a rule, had connexion with his female slaves. At all events, the early Middle Ages presents a state of things in which marriage was ecclesiastical rather than legal. It fell under the canon law, and not the common or statute law of the country. All formal marriage was ultimately abolished about the eleventh century in the case of the clergy, but this did not prevent them from having unwedded wives, or concubines, who, in some cases (e.g., in the kingdom of Naples) enjoyed, by express enactment, the same rights of immunity from secular jurisdiction, i.e., from the criminal law, as their partners. Even to this day in Spain and Italy, it is stated to be often made a condition of a priest occupying a certain curé that he should keep a concubine, with a view to the protection of the parishional wife and daughter.

The open and avowed freedom of the Middle Ages (a relic of the old group-marriage surviving possibly in the ius primae noctis) in the relations of the sexes, is a universally acknowledged fact. Ecclesiastical anathemas against fleshly lusts had little effect on the practice of men. Unfortunately, the freedom was often connected, as it always must be, where formal monogamy is maintained, with the breach of a plighted troth, that is to say, with deliberate deception. And this necessarily complicates the question from an ethical point of view, though the recognition of the fact by both parties may have tended to mitigate its evils. Neither in ancient nor in mediaeval times then has monogamy probably ever been any but a counsel of perfection, in ancient times only existing in the loosest and most conventional manner; and in mediaeval times, though exalted to the rank of a religious sacrament, never permanently maintained by public opinion in this exalted position, whatever may have been the case in sporadic outbursts. In the ancient world even the prostitute had often a high social position; in the Middle Ages incontinence was a sin to be purged by a slight penance; social ostracism, where it existed, confined apparently by a singular irony to the case of unmarried females.[2] But in this as in other matters the original Christian counsel of perfection present throughout the Middle Ages in the background, and ever and anon making itself felt in customs, institutions, and decrees gradually solidified as the barbaric element in mediaeval civilisation died down, and, in proportion as the middle classes rose to power, became permanently embodied in law and public opinion. Puritan sentiment was, of course, severely monogamic; and in the severity of the Protestant judgment of the "sin" of unchastity, we have the converging of two or three lines of thought.

The original Christian counsel of perfection was based on the notion that the relation between the sexes was symbolical of the mystical relation between the soul and the divinity, or in the form which it afterwards took between Christ and the Church. The sensual object thus fell into the background; marriage was only a toleration of the weakness of the natural man, as saith the Anglican marriage service. The notion of "purity" or abstinence from sexual intercourse as a sign of supreme virtue may be traced to three different co-operating factors –

1. the totemist or fetishistic worship of the sexual organs themselves – one of the earliest forms of the religious instinct, which took a variety of shapes being connected, sometimes it is true, with voluptuous rites, but also (e.g., the Syrian goddess) sometimes with ascetic rites;

2. the dualistic notion of the inherent evil of matter as opposed to the divine nature of spirit which was the speculative basis of this introspective morality of later times; and

149

3. the notion which grew up on this basis, that "holiness" consisted in the mortification of the individual, i.e., the natural man, his necessities and desires; in proportion as he overcame these being his approach to the divinity.

There exists to this day a sect of Hindoo Yogis who, in order that they may not enjoy the pleasures of eating and drinking, and at the same time may not lower the dignity of the divine nature within them by performing the lower animal functions, subsist on a little milk, which they leave in their stomachs for a while, until the system has absorbed sufficient nourishment to sustain life, and then throw up again by swallowing a ball with a string attached to it, thereby averting the necessity of its passing through their bodies. This is aptly characterised by the late Mr. King, in his work on The Gnostics, as "the finest possible reductio ad absurdum, of the notion of meritorious continence." These highly logical ascetics we commend to the serious attention of the Social Purity League, who are, we fear, as yet very far from the kingdom of heaven of true continence. Out of these three elements then is compounded the theoretical aspect of Protestant or. Puritan sexual morality. The last mentioned is deducible from the "Introspective" or individualistic ethics, which was the main element in Christian ethics.

But behind this speculative aspect of modern monogamic morality, is a very practical economic consideration, a consideration which has come to the fore in proportion as the belief in the speculative side of things has faded. The reverence of the bourgeois for the monogamic principle now rests almost entirely on the fact, that he objects to being exposed to the danger of having to put his hand in his pocket for the maintenance of his neighbours' children. This is the real core of "La morale bourgeoise." Now, in an individualistic society like ours, this sentiment is not, perhaps unnatural or particularly reprehensible, and it doubtless represents a very real difficulty in the solution of the problem, certainly under present and perhaps under imperfectly socialistic conditions. Clearly no one has a right to recklessly procreate children under circumstances like those of our present society without ensuring, as far as possible, their adequate support. Legalised monogamic marriage, it may be said, is some sort of check on this, and a fortiori, on possible demands on the ratepayer's pocket. Granted, so much, but let us have no cant in this matter.

In the present day there are but two alternatives – the mystical sanction of monogamy, and what we may term the vestryman sanction. The only rational position of those who take up the strict lines of legalised monogamic chastity and sniff disapprovingly at the fact, or the notion, of sexual intercourse outside this relation, is the mystical-christian sanction. Such a one must regard marriage and the sexual relation generally, as the sacred symbol of a solemn, mystical truth, otherwise he is a blatant fraud. For though he may "most powerfully and potently" believe in the economic or vestryman sanction, yet this alone, while it might lead to reasoned remonstrance, could not possibly evoke any genuine unction of the kind one is accustomed to associate with conventional laudations of chastity, and condemnations of its breach, or with finger-pointings at the non-respectable woman. For this sanction has a quite, peculiar flavour, which could in reality only be caused by an outrage on our deepest feelings, such as would rend our hearts, and not merely by one that might possibly rend our trousers-pockets. The unctuous saint, if we are persuaded of his sincerity, one may respect and even love, but the unctuous vestryman no man can love. Besides, the "vestryman" sanction – that is the one consisting of mere economical expediency – loses its direct force in at least two cases within the limits of our present society. It loses it where the question of offspring is eliminated by "practical malthusianism," or other causes; it loses it where the offspring are as well provided for as they would be in marriage. It loses it, as a matter of course, when the economic basis of society, from being individualistic, has become socialistic. The vestryman or trousers-pocket sanction of marriage is, therefore, obviously not of a nature to give the institution a fundamental ethical basis, and hence, we are justified in saying that monogamy as an ethical principle collapses with the collapse of theological mysticism. For this reason, the various Christian sects are trying to constitute themselves the custodians of monogamy and the conventional sexual morality, as the only remunerative occupation left them, except philanthropy after the loss of public interest in God and Christ.

In addition to the Christians there are the Positivists and miscellaneous rhetoricians who seek to prop up monogamy by phrases. They are, however, a very feeble folk, so far as this question is concerned. We have already pointed out the only two solid arguments for the monogamic principle and the sexual abstinence it involves. Now, these good people can't exactly accept either the "mystical" or the "vestryman" position. Hence, they take refuge in deliciously vague declamation on the nobility, on the loftiness, of the ideal which handcuffs one man and one woman together for life We are never allowed to see precisely where the nobility and the loftiness come in, but we are assured that they are there. The mere commonplace man, if left to himself, would probably think that it rested entirely upon circumstances, upon character, temperament, and whether the perpetual union of two persons was desirable. There are excellent men and women (possibly the majority) born with dispositions for whom a single permanent union is doubtless just the right thing; there are other excellent men and women who are born with lively imaginations and bohemian temperaments for whom it is not always precisely the right thing. Now, the plain man of ordinary reflection would imagine that all there phases of human nature have their justification and their corresponding ideals. No, says the Positivist, or other rhetorical upholder of strict monogamy, there is only one absolute ideal, and on to the procrustean bed of this ideal all men and women must be stretched. An admirable specimen of this school of windy rhetoric is to be found in an article on marriage by Miss A. Chapman in the Westminster Review for April, 1889. This interesting young lady would apparently modify the institution of matrimony in the sense of making it absolutely indissoluble on the one hand and on the other by making the woman supreme dictator! Then she thinks we should have ideal marriage! Of course, there is the usual rant about the individual who would be prejudiced by this beautiful arrangement (a rather large number we are afraid), sacrificing himself for the good of the whole, which we are exhorted to believe, on the strength of much tall writing, is inextricably bound up with it. The good of the whole, forsooth! as if it were possible for an institution which admittedly, in the natural course of things, must breed suffering for individuals can, by any possibility, be for the good of the whole! It may be the duty of the individual an special occasions to sacrifice himself for the happiness of the "whole," but that is a very different thing from his sacrificing himself on behalf of an institution which involves, in its essential nature, a perpetual sacrifice for those that succeed him. For how could a society in which such an institution existed be either a healthy or a happy one, either as a whole or for the individual? If this be not so, it is clearly the duty of every individual to protest against it openly by word and deed, rather than for the sake of gaining the applause of mawkish sentimentalists to sanction it either by speech or action.

Herein we have an instance of the distinction between bourgeois morality and socialist morality. To the first it is "immoral" to live in a marital relation without having previously subscribed to certain legal formalities, but it is perfectly "moral" to stifle conviction, or to act against conviction, for the sake of worldly advantage, to enter the Church without believing in its dogmas, to enter the army and serve in wars which your conscience disapproves, to embark in journalism mid advocate political or other views you really despise, because it answers your purpose. To the second these are the things that defile a man, but to live in a state of unlegalised marriage defileth not a man, "nor woman neither." There are some persons even, who need enjoining to deny themselves the pleasures of asceticism and the smug self-satisfaction they derive from it.

There is a good deal of talk about marriage as the union of two souls, etc., and many men, on the strength of this, endeavour to persuade themselves that they really find their wives' society and converse interesting and elevating. By this and similar subterfuges they try to embellish and cover up the gross physical fact which it expresses. That in a few cases, social intercourse is the most prominent motive in marriage we would not for a moment deny, but in nine cases out of ten the assumption of its existence is a pious fraud which the modern man of culture practices upon himself. Who has not suffered from the wives of friends? In the present day, with notions in the air of the equality of the sexes, a man's friend is apt to require him to enjoy his wife's society as much as his own, which is rather hard. For one may be quite prepared to love one's neighbour, but yet may strongly resent having to love one's neighbour's wife as well. With the husband the sexual interest covers up the intellectual vacuity; but, unluckily, his friend sees everything in its true colour. As a matter of fact, no man who can get men's society straightaway desires women's, for he says men's is better. Hence the institution of the "club" in this country and the "cafe" on the continent. The efforts of noble-minded men who try to find something intellectually interesting in the subject of their monogamy when there is nothing, though perhaps a praiseworthy discipline, are exceedingly painful to the onlooker.

Enforced monogamy and its correlate, prostitution, is the great historical antithesis of civilisation in the sexual sphere, just as mastership and service is in the economic sphere, or as God and nature in the speculative sphere, or as sin and holiness in the sphere of ethics generally. The group-marriage promiscuity of primitive barbaric society is as far removed from prostitution as from compulsory monogamy. With the rise of private-property holding and of cities, monogamy and prostitution tended to supervene over group marriage. This antithesis is the negation of group-marriage; in proportion as group-marriage disappears it obtains pre-eminence. Socialism will strike at the root at once of compulsory monogamy and of prostitution by inaugurating an era of marriage based on free choice and intention, and characterised by the absence of external coercion. For where the wish for the maintenance of the marriage-relation remains, there external compulsion is unnecessary; where it is necessary, because the wish has disappeared, there it is undesirable. The above is all we can foresee in the matter.

In this, as in other departments, the modern man, immersed in the categories of the bourgeois world, sees everything through them. For him, therefore, there exists only legalised monogamic marriage and prostitution, both of which are based essentially on commercial considerations. The one is purchase, the other hire. He cannot see the higher and only really moral form of the marriage-relation which transcends both, and which is based neither on sale nor hire. Prostitution is immoral as implying the taking advantage by the woman of a monopoly which costs her no labour for the sake of extorting money from the man. But the condition of legal marriage – maintenance – does the same.

If it be asked, is marriage a failure? the answer of any impartial person must be – monogamic marriage is a failure – the

155

rest is silence. We know not what new form of the family the society of the future, in which men and woman will be alike economically, free, may evolve, and which may be generally adopted therein. Meanwhile, we ought to combat by every means within our power the metaphysical dogma of the inherent sanctity of the monogamic principle. Economic development on the one side, and the free initiative of individuals on the other, will do the rest.

Notes

1. By the word "monogamy," as used below, is to be understood not merely the union either temporary or permanent of one man with one woman, but such union plus some form of legal compulsion or interference other than that which obtains in ordinary cases of contract.

2. This is the case still in many parts of the Continent of Europe, where the cachet of being a legal wife or widow covers a multitude of irregularities.

III

9. Courage

The Logic, Phenomenology, and History of a Concept
(May 1890)

How shall we define Courage? What do we mean by Courage? Let us seek the broadest expression possible of courage – the bare notion of courage in itself. So considered, may we not define it as the subordination of pain or fear to resolution or purpose? I can think of no more catholic definition in words of the notion than this one, or one that more completely excludes all debatable matter as to the extent of the operation of will, or the degree of consciousness of the purpose, involved in "true" courage, still less ulterior considerations of the content of the purpose. No one would call the indifference to danger of an infant or an idiot, or the mere endurance of the man powerless to resist, courage, but some might affirm that certain animals could be said to have courage, or that the mere physical absence of fear would constitute a claim to the possession of courage, and many other such things. Again, no one would say that to jump over a precipice without an object was a brave action. Let us take this, then, as the primary abstract definition of courage per se – the subordination of pain or fear to resolution or purpose. The corresponding formula for cowardice will, of course, be the opposite of this – the subordination of resolution or purpose to pain or fear. But though there is a formal opposition here, there is no real opposition. Courage and cowardice are absolutely indistinguishable from this point of view. Thus, a man, shall we say, fights to the death rather than runs away. But why does he fight rather than run away? Is the doing so courage, or is it cowardice? Does he fight because he is a brave man, and does not fear death? Or does he fight the rather because he is a coward, and fears the derision of public opinion which would follow on his running away? It is conceivable that, a man of little imagination, he fears Mrs. Grundy, whom he knows personally, more than the "king of terrors," whom he does not. Or, take the case of the suicide. He does not fear death, a great terror to many, but yet he is called a coward by the man of correct morals because he fears to encounter the troubles of life. Of course, the man of correct morals is here only making believe; he does not really think the suicide a coward, but it is the proper thing to say in the interests of conventional morality, and a rather nice doctrine for himself, too, inasmuch as he probably fears the troubles of life less than death, and therefore he, Q.E.D., is a brave man. But even though he may be shamming, the logic of the man of correct morals is unimpeachable. He has a perfect right, from a theoretical point of view, to take up the position he does. Considered in their most abstract expressions, courage and cowardice are indistinguishable. There is no outward mark by which we can affirm, on the strength of the mere abstract definition of courage or cowardice, that a particular action is courageous or the reverse.

In the case of the man who fights and runs away, it is impossible to say that he is not actually showing courage – i.e., subordinating fear to resolution in running away. He may run away from an overwhelming sense of the duty of preserving himself to fight another day. It may have cost him a stupendous moral effort to resolve to run away and face the ridicule and the contumely of his fellows rather than yield to his inclination as a fighting man to hold on and die with harness on his back. It may cost a man no effort to fight and much to run away, or it may cost no effort to run away and much to fight. There is possible fear on either side; there is possible resolution on either side. So that the bare abstract conceptions of courage and cowardice are, when applied to the concrete world, perfectly interchangeable. We must first have a concrete and particular case before us before we can determine motive, and hence before we can predicate courage or cowardice of any action. To fight is usually regarded as a brave action, to run away as a cowardly action; but, as we have shown, the reverse may just as easily be the case. All actions to which the pair of concepts – courage and cowardice – are applicable at all, may, in short, fall under one or the other indifferently; there being no action absolutely brave as such, and no action absolutely cowardly as such. The distinction between the concepts – courage and cowardice – is as yet formal and not real. All this is no mere logomachy, but very important, inasmuch as there are few ethical concepts with which the general public are so fond of playing fast and loose as with this one, and their ability to do so rests on the arbitrary application of the concept in its purely formal aspect as though it were a real one.

We now come to the distinction between moral and physical courage. Here we are concerned with the degrees of consciousness of purpose involved in the act of resolution – i.e., in how far it is an act of individual initiation, properly so-called, and in how far merely the spontaneous effervescence of animal spirits. Reflecting on courage, we find that this distinction is involved therein. The question is no longer merely the subordinating of pain or fear to resolution or purpose, which always presents itself in a double aspect, the possible fear and the possible resolution being assumable on either side, but the definiteness of the resolution, the steadfastness, clearness, and rationality with which the purpose is conceived. This latter is not double-sided. Physical courage is always implicitly or explicitly distinguishable from moral courage in all actions into which the category of courage enters. Assume the courage, and the action itself tells you whether it is physical or moral. To take an obvious, if somewhat homely illustration. When the peasant or Donnybrook Irishman goes forth to punch a head in general, regardless of the result upon his own, he shows physical courage;

159

but when the Irish member, in the full swing of the London season, deliberately, after weeks of reflection, bears the obloquy of the police court and punches the head of a particularly obnoxious member of a Tory Government, he may be doing a foolish and even an improper thing, but he shows moral courage. The Donnybrook Irishman has made the resolution to exercise his muscles in a particular manner, and to this resolution he subordinates the fear of personal injury to himself. But the resolution here is more instinctive than conscious, and not the result of deliberate resolution. The mere sense of physical power is sufficient to effect it. In the other case, on the contrary, it is not the result of an animal instinct but of an intellectual act. The resolution here does not come of itself, but is created and sustained by a conscious and definite act of will of the individual as such. We see in this second stage of the analysis that an opposition has arisen within the concept. It has sucked up the contradiction into itself. In the first place we had only to deal with the external opposition of courage and cowardice. Now we have to do with an internal opposition, that between physical, animal, or instinctive courage, in which the resolution and the purpose arise without any effort on the part of the individual as the mere result of his inherited animal, system, and moral courage, in which the purpose and the resolution are created and framed by the intellect and will of the individual himself. Animal courage, though it may evoke a kind of aesthetic admiration can never evoke moral praise properly so-called. For animal courage is outside the sphere of individual initiation, which consists in definite choice and not in natural impulse. Animal courage involves no effort, because the fear is not felt or the danger realised.

The natural impulse and all those elements in his character which form part of the Logic of Nature are necessary and imposed upon the individual; it is the particular or individual element par excellence as opposed to this universal element, that

160

which constitutes his particularity or his thisness, which is the decisive factor. But the thisness, the hereness and nowness, is the illogical and irrational element in all Reality, and always opposes itself to the universal or logical element. It is the Hyle which is as yet not Ousia. The much-vaunted freewill is nothing but the illogical or irrational element in the essence of the individual, his undetermined particularity, as opposed to the logical element, or that in him which is universal and necessary. The former corresponds to chance in external nature; it is the element which is transient and irreducible to law. But it is, nevertheless, this element alone, the alogical spontaneity or thisness of the individual in the act of rationalising himself, which with doubtful accuracy we term freewill, with which moral praise or blame is concerned. You can only praise or blame this particular man for that in him which concerns his thisness or his particularity. The other spontaneity which is not identified with effort on the part of the individual is reducible to so-called natural law. Moral courage must then involve an effort of individual initiation which may or may not be accompanied by physical or animal courage. The subordination of fear to resolution must take place through an individual nisus here and now and not through an irresponsible impulse. The opposition between physical and moral courage is sometimes realised in a striking manner, as in the case of that Russian bureaucrat spoken of by Stepniak who sheltered the Nihilist, though the doing so plunged him into an abyss of terror himself. The extreme form of moral courage brings us to the question of how far individual interest in the object of the resolution to which present fear or pain is subordinated is compatible with courage. That it is not involved in the primary definition of courage is obvious, but on reflection the general conscience of mankind proclaims that the fullest expression of moral courage is reached when pain or fear is subordinated, not to the purpose of individual advantage, but to a purely disinterested end. For the subordination of the individual to the purpose then becomes complete. It is not merely immediate fear or pain which is subordinated in the resolution, but the whole content of the individuality is staked upon something, the interest of which is outside itself. The Oriental who braves death or torture rather than divulge to a rapacious tax-gatherer his hidden store of wealth, or the prize-fighter who exposes his life for a stake of money may show a kind of courage which we instinctively accept as such; but the man who plunges into a burning building, and falling rafters, and suffocating smoke, to save a stranger's life, our reason accepts as showing a higher, more perfect and complete kind of courage. That the fullest manifestations of moral courage presuppose the disposition to physical courage is a proposition hardly admitting of a doubt. A fine kind of courage may be shown, like that of the Russian Bureaucrat above referred to, in passivity, but it is one-sided; the completest manifestations of courage involve an activity, and to "deeds of heroism" the mere physical disposition is requisite. Stepniak's Russian, though exhibiting the highest moral courage in sheltering his friend, while so keenly feeling the sense of his own danger, might, nevertheless, owing to his lack of mere animal courage, have fallen a victim to panic had he been set to lead a forlorn hope. The completest form of courage, then, may be defined as the subordination of pain or fear to a resolution involving a disinterested object, and realising itself indifferently whether in action or passion.

The last definition, introducing, as it does, the question of content, brings us to the threshold of the concrete world. We have now traced three distinct phases in the concept courage. The first was the mere definition, vague as regards all content, "The subordination of fear to purpose." The second, the well-known distinction between physical and moral courage, was in apparent contradiction with the primary definition, inasmuch as in physical courage which is, per se, purely active in its manifestations, the action seems the result of blind instinct (as in the case of the Donnybrook Irishman), and it is only on reflection that we discover the implicit motive (to wit, in this case, the need for muscular exertion); while in moral courage, which is, per se, purely passive in its manifestations, the fear does not always, at first sight, seem subordinated (as in the case of Stepniak's Russian), and it is only reflection which shows us that the man, though he trembled for his own safety, was no coward, but brave, since the fear itself was in essence fully subordinated by a conscious effort to the end in view. Reflection further impels us to introduce into our definition of courage the nature of the object (as to whether disinterested or not), in addition to bringing to light the one-sided nature alike of physical and moral courage considered per se, and thus introduces the concluding definition of courage in which the vagueness of the primary form of the concept and the one-sidedness of the secondary form are alike abolished, while the essential determinations of both these forms are maintained.

The phenomenology of courage exhibits some curious combinations and a good many spurious modes. There is the apparent courage of the man who is insensible to danger, not because he subordinates fear to purpose, but because he lacks imagination, or because his imagination is blunted in particular directions through custom, or because, maybe, he is ignorant of the danger threatening him. There is no real subordination of fear to purpose in any of these cases. Thus (to take an example referred to by Aristotle) the seaman does not fear a storm as the landsman does, because he may have confidence in the steersman or the goodness of his ship, or what not; or because, having passed through many storms unscathed, his imagination has got blunted as to storms in general. The landsman may think him brave, when in reality he is not so. Let us suppose the landsman is a physician, and he takes the sea-captain through a cholera hospital or through a leper-house; while the physician walks unmoved, taking a purely scientific interest in all he sees around him, the mariner may in his turn quake with fear and turn pale. On the other hand, the seaman may fear a certain course while the landsman sees the vessel taking that course unmoved, not because the seaman is more timid than the landsman, but simply because he foresees a special danger attending it unknown to the latter. The landsman's unmoved bearing while the ship is being driven straight upon shoals, looks like that form of moral courage which consists in the subordination of fear to personal dignity, or the evoking for one's person of the admiration of others – and which is shown in the suppression of the outward manifestations of the unpleasant – while in reality it is nothing of the kind, but the mere insensibility of ignorance.

Then, again, the boor or the idiot, whose imaginative powers are sluggish, will never have the idea of future danger present to him, because be never has ideas at all, and is incapable of receiving any vivid or lasting impression on his imagination. Such an insensible person will seem brave, but not be so. His imaginative power is so feeble that only a very present pain or a most immediate danger can affect him. It requires intellect to be intelligently afraid.

The secret of a good deal of apparent courage lies in this: Most persons are afraid of something, but they, at times, show up brave on the background of persons who are afraid of something else. For some reason or other, inherited or acquired, a particular thing affects the imagination of some persons more powerfully, they realise it more graphically, than others. I knew a man in Berlin, who had been through the Franco-German War, had fought at Gravelotte, seen thousands fall around him at Sedan, had stormed the trenches of Metz, and been made a sergeant on account of his services in the field, who yet quailed before the sting of a gnat. His hand became slightly inflamed, and he was thrown into a paroxysm of fear of blood-poisoning. I saw him deadly white and trembling and scarcely able to walk from fright. What mitrailleuses, Gatlings, and chassepots were unable to effect, that did a little summer fly. A friend of mine who fears neither infection, nor mad dogs, nor infuriated bulls, in fly-time is prostrated with terror at the presence of a wasp round about his person. All men may seem brave in disposition until their Achilles-heel is disclosed. The seeming coward is often merely a man of exceptionally vivid imagination, the seeming brave man often merely one of dull imagination.

A more specious form of spurious courage than those already mentioned is the performance of an act apparently, but not really, involving danger. For example, a woman in the present day who throws herself in front of a squadron of dragoons to stem their passage, or tries to force her way through a cordon of police, performs an act which in a man would be courageous, and she wins an additional kudos from the popular opinion as to the weakness of her sex. But in reality, this very opinion is her protection, and deprives the action of all special claim to heroism. She knows the dragoons will not disembowel her with their bayonets; she knows the policemen will not brain her with their truncheons. Her "womanhood" is a sufficient protection for her. Certain women in the past, as Jeanne d'Arc, the Maid of Saragossa, &c., in a time when women did not enjoy the privileged immunities exacted by modern sentiment, have really shown heroism in braving dangers which were as real for them as for men. The same may be said of certain women during the final struggle of the Commune, in 1871, when for the nonce class-ferocity overrode class-gallantry. It is strange, by the way, that in modern warfare the exploitation of the above sentiment has never been tried by the losing side. A reserve corps of Amazons suddenly intercepted between an attacking and a defending force, might easily save the latter from a disastrous rout. Flaubert describes how the "mercenary" Matho protected himself from the missiles of the enraged Carthaginians by covering himself with the stolen veil of the moon-goddess as with a shield, none daring to violate the sacred vestment. So here, a regiment having fought a good fight, and being hard pressed, might effect a secure and orderly retreat, having drawn around itself the protecting veil of its reserve womanhood. The attacking body must instantly fall back, unable to follow up their antagonists. Military men possibly consider, however, that the difficulties of training the Amazonian "cover" would be insuperable.

There is another form of spurious or, at least, of cheap bravery which is connected with the foregoing subject. In a domestic squabble, such as may from time to time be seen in some of the bye-ways of London, in which a man and his wife are engaged, the passer-by, greedy of renown for street prowess, will ostentatiously stalk up to the disputants, and without informing himself further in the matter, will take the part of the woman and commence objurgating and possibly threatening the man. He thinks to obtain credit for pluck and determination for championing what is conventionally supposed to be the weaker side. He knows all the time that he will probably have the bystanding profanum vulgus on his side, and that the unlucky husband will be quite unable to retaliate upon him for the insults received. Were he to take the side of the man he might have to face half-a-dozen other individuals equally desirous with himself of acquiring the local and temporary renown of the street. But this might be unpleasant, and more than that renown was worth, and would require pluck indeed. Similarly, the murderer of a seducer, though he often poses as a hero, really knows that he may rely on the support of a clamorous and often hypocritical section of public opinion.

By taking the mere phenomenal aspect of courage in abstraction from the concept, which it presupposes, it is easy to degrade the terminology of courage to silly and meaningless epithets of abuse, and this is commonly done.

Courage in its manifestations involves the encountering of pain or danger. But courage does not mean the mere encountering pain or danger. Every sane person would regard the man who, without any object, even that of suicide, tried to cross and recross a railway line before an express train only two or three hundred yards distant in the off-chance of accomplishing the feat safely, as a lunatic or a fool. There must be some conceivably adequate motive to stamp the encountering of danger as the manifestation of courage. Now it is a common trick to postulate some sentiment or whim of A as an adequate motive for B to encounter pain or danger, and the refusal to do so is stigmatised by B as cowardice. A good instance of this is to be found in the dog-muzzling controversy. A well-known authoress, famed for her erotic novels, zealously contends for the freedom of every mangy cur to bite how, when, and where it pleases. Being unable to support this contention by any valid argument, she falls back on the rather stale device of stigmatising those persons who are sane enough to object to unlimited freedom of biting as cowards. The contention is, of course, that the trifling inconvenience which the muzzle causes the cur, in preventing him from exercising his natural proclivity to bite, should supply an adequate motive for the man to run the risk of being bitten. Those who would take steps to restrain the mordant liberty of the cur, since they do not hold the doctrine of the divine right of dogs to bite just because it is their nature to, think that sentimental scruples as to muzzling them are evidence, not so much of natural courage as of native imbecility.

Or to take another instance. A neighbour practises sparrow-shooting in his back garden while I am sitting at my window writing. About every sixth time he fires, the shot whizzes around my head; the remainder of the shot is distributed between the upper air and other neighbour's windows. I, in common with those others, object to the practice. It is true that only at about every sixth discharge of the gun the shot comes in at my window at all, and even then it may not touch me, since the space

167

occupied by the window is many times that occupied by my head. But, nevertheless, I join in the general protest. We don't say that we think anything of the danger, but we insist on the practice being stopped on the ground that there is a lady in delicate health who is prejudicially affected by the noise, just as people never mind going into a house where there is scarlet fever or small-pox on their own account, but only through fear of carrying the infection to their families. Our garden sportsman, however, thinks he sees through us. After some excited discussion, indignant at having his sport abolished, he looks us full in the face, and says: "The fact is, you're a pack of d—d cowards; you're afraid of being shot, that's what it is!" Now it is not nice to be called a coward, and after this who could refuse to show his pluck by allowing the sparrow-shooter to continue as before? Just as "Ouida" considers that the pleasure the canine race in general takes in being free to bite, or perhaps the trouble it gives her to keep her dogs muzzled (as the case may be), a sufficient reason for men repressing their natural dislike to being bitten by mad dogs, so the sparrow-shooter thinks the pleasure he takes in his sport an adequate ground for his neighbours repressing their natural disinclination to their persons becoming the possible objective of small shot. The term "coward" is thus degraded to a mere abusive epithet based on individual caprice.

In the history of the concept courage, we have the logical determinations of courage realised or manifested in concreto. The mere logical determinations per se are abstract, the mere phenomenal manifestations per se are also abstract. The concept, though imbedded in them, is only discernible on analysis. In History, on the other hand, which, while no abstraction, is in its true sense an ideal reproduction of a reality in which the unessential is left out, and therefore no mere summary of particular facts or phenomena, the concept is realised – clothed in flesh and blood. The first period in the development of human society exhibits courage in its pure and immediate form, unconscious of itself as such. The clansman or tribesman fights for his kinship-group because he cannot conceive of doing otherwise. He lives only in it and through it. Fear is with him, unconsciously but uninterruptedly subordinated to a purpose of which he is perhaps also only vaguely conscious, and the consciousness of the fear and the purpose first become apparent on the decay of tribal society, when it is approaching the transition to civilisation. It is to this period that the great epics of the world belong. In the Iliad, in Beowulf, in the Scandinavian sagas, we see courage first recognising and admiring itself as such and holding, as it were, a mirror up to itself. Human society had existed, thousands of men had fought and died for tribe and kindred, but none had been found to sing their acts. Human society was unconscious of itself. It had not as yet become object to itself. Just as in logic, every real concept is but the reproduction of the abstract elements it presupposes; as in psychology every time-moment of our life contains the presentment not of itself, but of the moment passing away or just past; so in history it is a society in the act of passing away, which first knows itself as it is in itself. The nameless epic singer is the expression of this self-consciousness as regards primitive society. Courage and valorous deeds are the object of his lay, as they it is which strike the awakening consciousness of society most. It is now that the distinction between courage and cowardice manifests itself. The first mention of cowardice in literature is in the 6th book of the Iliad, i.e., the Dolon incident. It is as yet a sporadic abnormity scarcely conceivable to the average man. The appearance of cowardice is one of the symptoms of the dawn of civilisation, and the first faint glimmerings of introspection.

Tribal Society becomes conscious of itself, and embodies that consciousness in the epic long before the individual becomes conscious of himself as having interests apart from the society. This latter consciousness – that of the opposition of the individual and society – brings to light the further distinction between

169

physical courage and moral courage. The old courage, however, the courage which knows no cowardice – much less the opposition between physical and moral – lingers on in a bastard form in the mercenary soldier of antiquity and other historical periods. The opposition of physical or active and moral or passive courage is the cardinal form of the concept courage throughout the period of civilisation. Most manifestations of courage, most dispositions to courage, fall under one of these heads to the exclusion of the other, or at least the unequal balancing of the two is observable. The classical instance of moral courage is that of the endurance of the early Christians. Determination such as that described in the Acts of the Martyrs of Lyons, even if we allow a margin for exaggeration, implies a moral courage quantitatively unsurpassed. But we cannot reckon the endurance of the early Christian Martyrs to the highest forms of moral courage qualitatively, for the simple reason that its purpose was not disinterested. A firm belief in death being the portal of eternal bliss and glory, in golden cities, in great white thrones sustained these martyrs. The purpose, therefore, to which pain or fear was subordinated was that of direct personal advantage or reward, the same in kind as that of the Oriental who endures tortures rather than divulge his hidden store of wealth to the tax-gatherer. Moral courage has probably both quantitatively and qualitatively reached its highest point in the Russian revolutionary movement of our own day. Here the greatest conceivable suffering is endured for ends which are absolutely impersonal.

We see, then, courage opposing itself first to cowardice as in the grey dawn of History society first becomes conscious of itself through the individuals composing it. Afterwards as the individual and his interests become separated from, and gain the upper hand over, the society and its interests, and with that introspective habit of mind which follows more or less closely thereupon, courage falls asunder into physical (generally coincident with active) and moral (generally coincident with passive) courage. This opposition is characteristic of civilisation, and in an advanced civilisation it is the exception to find a man in whom moral and physical courage are indissolubly blended.

But what as to the future of courage? In a society in which present economical conditions are changed, and in which an equal possibility of development is ensured for each and all alike – what form will courage take? We cannot, indeed, expect a recrudescence of that undefined, perhaps, but all-pervading enthusiasm which sent forth the man of the early world to fight for race and kindred, not knowing himself as personality distinct from them, a courage differing from physical courage as such, inasmuch as it was no mere effervescence of animal spirits, and yet differing from moral courage as such, inasmuch as no conscious effort was involved in it. But yet with men living a healthy life, physically and mentally, who can doubt that our present opposition between physical and moral courage will give place to a different and an intrinsically higher courage than any that have hitherto obtained, a courage according with the changed conditions, a courage no longer displaying itself, indeed, as in the onrush of the barbaric foeman, or the endurance of the martyr, the necessity for such having passed away, but in other ways – a courage less outwardly brilliant perhaps, but even more real, because more constant in its disinterestedness of purpose, and more sustained in the definiteness with which that purpose is conceived?

E. Belfort Bax

[The Editor takes this opportunity of reminding the

readers of Time that all signed articles are on the same footing, and that the writer alone is responsible for any opinions expressed in them. The Editor in taking a place among the signed contributors in so doing divests himself pro hac vice of his official character and becomes as one of them. – Editor of Time]

10. The Practical Significance of Philosophy

(December 1890)

The Philistine said all metaphysics is a snare and a delusion. Mathematics is the only abstract study worth pursuing. Metaphysics deals with subjects outside the range of human ken; it is simply baseless thinking on that which we can never know, etc., etc. All this sort of talk may be had at a very low rate, even without the asking, from any callow young man of the middle classes who has a little smattering of modern »culture.« But let us for once »odi« this »profanem vulgus,« let us clear our minds of the cant of metaphysicophobia for the nonce, and let us see if this thing, despised and rejected of practical men, can possibly have any practical significance or not.

Philosophy or metaphysics, it is said, deals with things outside the range of human experience. Does it? It is important to rid ourselves of this popular superstition at the outset. The main problem of speculative philosophy, since Kant, has been to analyse experience or common-sense reality into its simplest elements, to discover the ultimate condition which each plane of experience presupposes, and first of all the ultimate condition which all experience presupposes, since without this last we can have no clue to guide us in our ulterior investigations. Philosophy knows nothing of outside experience. For philosophy is nothing more than the consideration and comprehension of experience or reality from a new point of view, that is, a point of view differing as essentially from that of science as from that of so-called common-sense. The first thing, then, we have to ask ourselves in entering upon philosophical investigation is – what is the element or material common to all reality? What is the warp out of which

173

all experience is woven? What does all experience presuppose? This is really a very simple question in itself, notwithstanding the vastness of the issues it opens up. The warp of which reality[1] consists cannot be space or extension, for this is a mere blank form of external objects; it cannot be matter (in the physical sense), for this is merely a name for a synthesis of qualities in space which are perceived or thought, and which have no meaning apart from their perceivedness, as old Berkeley showed it cannot be mind, for this is made up of »impressions and ideas« derived from external experience, or, in other words, from the physical universe. (Heste, Locke and the empirical psychologists.) Lastly, it cannot be time, for this is also merely a blank form of concrete objects external and internal, or, in short, of things physical and psychical, and although it is thus in a sense common to all reality, it does not constitute any positive element in the constitution of reality. Time, moreover, itself presupposes an apprehending of itself; it is not self-subsistent. What then is more fundamental than all these? The answer is the act of apprehension. All object, all existence, no less the things of the world than our own mental states − is an apprehension, a bethought feeling, or, in other words, feeling shot with thought. But we have not yet quite got to the root of the matter. For the apprehension is a synthesis, and may be analysed. All actual apprehension or concrete consciousness presupposes the power or possibility of apprehension, or, in other words, that which apprehends. But this ground of all apprehension is obviously nothing else than the »I« from which the apprehension, the awareness, the consciousness wells up. »I« is at once the ground and raw material of reality. Though it identifies itself perpetually with a definite and particular series of mental states bound together by a memory-synthesis and called myself or this personality, it is nevertheless the eternal background of consciousness in general. Now this indefinite and immediate thatness or nisus, which is the »I« in its pure form, the Subject par excellence (and to which, indeed, the latter word can alone be properly applied), is, from this point of view, a mere inchoate abstractum. Feeler and feeling are at this stage undistinguished; we have a mere thatness per se, which is absurd and as such involves its own negation, i.e., the undifferentiated feeling implies feltness. The »I« per se, the matter, is negated or determined (omnis determinato est negatio) as feltness or whatness, as the form of externality, as not-itself, as not-I, but this negation in its turn evinces itself as untenable. Feltness is not self-subsistent, but is thrown back on the »I« or Subject as recognising itself as feeling, i.e., as distinguishing itself as feeling from its feltness, and in so far negating the form of externality. Now, this act of distinction is the most fundamental, the most universal expression of the logical synthesis – the immediate condition of concrete consciousness or knowledge. Immediately it is consciousness; or in reflection it is reason or knowledge. Abstract the differentia of the last term of the process from those which it presupposes, and you have »pure thought,« the »pure relation« of Hegel. Treated in this way, however, it becomes mere abstraction, and the conditions of a real synthesis, which always involve a double, alogical element (sense and its ground, the inner feeling and the outer felt, the that and the what), in addition to this logical element, are absent, an absence which cannot be atoned for by the plausible manipulation of pure thought-forms or categories.

Thus the primordial subject, the »I,« considered as pure inness or immediateness in its pure form, together with its negative, feltness, the distinguishing feature of which is outness, likewise immediate, both become mediated by the negation of the latter as such, and the re-assertion of the »I,« no longer as pure, but as limited or related to its opposite feltness, the that becomes related to the what, and this relation constitutes thought, which dominates all reality and interprets the whole process in its own terms. Thought is consciousness, in posse, consciousness is thought, in actu. This primal synthesis, as constituting the innermost nature of reality, that is, of experience or

175

consciousness-in-general (possible and actual), is involved throughout its whole range, for it alone constitutes reality. To employ the usual terminology, the essence of every real qua real consists in these three elements or momenta, a thatness or matter (=»I«), a whatness or form (= negation of »I« or feltness), and the limitation of each by each, whence results the relation or logical category, which, so to say, suffuses with its light the alogical process behind it, which it completes. Every real contains a non-rational as well as a rational element. This is the truth at the bottom of the »thing-in-itself,« so much decried by the orthodox Hegelians. To treat the thing-in-itself as a thing existing and yet independent of all possible apprehension is, of course, absurd. But it is scarcely more absurd than the reduction of reality to a mere logical process, a mere thinking and nothing more. (pace, T.H. Green Prologomena, passim.) We recognise this to be the case when we speak of the being of things, which always means that element in their reality which is not actually present in consciousness, what is present being merely the phenomenon or sign of the being or of the thatness which itself ever eludes us. (See Handbook to the History of Philosophy, 2nd Ed., Appendix.) The logical form is always statical, it is a fixating, a defining of things, while the strictly dynamical element in the real is always incapable of comprehension under logical forms – it is infinite. The one is being, the other thought. The purest product of thought – of the logical – is the concept form, that of mere relation. But under that general concept are embraced an infinite possibility of particulars, none of which completely realise the ideal form. The common illustration of this is the geometrical concept – point, straight line, surface, etc. – which is recognised as unrealisable. But the foregoing applies not only to the abstract concept – the concept that is without connotation, of which the geometrical is an instance – but also to the most concrete of concepts – man, horse, tree, etc.; the individual falling under the concept never completely realising the definition as such (that is, it in purity and perfection), but always adding to, or modifying it, so that each particular, or individual within the class in question, must have its

176

own concept, embracing its own differentia, the hierarchy of concepts extending to infinity in accordance with the potential infinity of individuation itself, if we are to regard the concept-form as ultimate. This is, of course, substantially the Aristotelian argument against the ideal theory. The rock on which all the great synthetic philosophical systems, from Plato to Hegel, have struck, has been the ignoring or the minimising of the fact that reality – the concrete synthesis – as such, necessarily involves an element of unreason, and that this element is as essential therein as that of reason. If this be admitted, and it is admitted incidentally even by Hegel, who in the main seeks to extrude it, it follows that Panlogism is a dream – a dream with which is connected, we may remark by the way, the attempt to give completion and finality to philosophical systems.

We must frankly admit then that Being can never be finally absorbed in Knowledge, can never be completely reduced to rationality, although Being apart from Knowledge is as unreal an abstraction as Knowledge apart from Being. Knowledge, the logical, must, it is true, be of the same »stuff« as Being, the alogical. Being (as objectivity) is simply transfigured I-ness (if I may borrow a terms used in another connexion), yet knowledge is none the less a reflected form of the »I,« the final condition of the realisation of the »I.« To Hegel[2] thought was ultimate, the »I« itself was merely a form of thought, and, as such, he was bound to reduce the alogical to terms of the logical.

But his failure is conspicuous in many places, and in none more than in the philosophy of Nature, where he has continually to slur over the element of chance and irrationality in Nature under the somewhat meaningless expression »ohnmacht« – the admission of which contradicts the assumption made at starting. He feels, that under the assumption of the perfect rationality of the real, he is compelled to set aside the alogical,, wherever it presents itself, with a stroke of the pen. The great master of speculation has earned the immortal glory of providing for us a scheme with which to work, but it is a scheme which must be rectified by restoring the elements neglected by him on account of the assumption with which lie set out, that know-ledge was all in all, that the differentia of the final term of the synthesis of the real (of the concrete) annihilated rather than transformed the momenta it presupposes, that they were merely forms of it rather than that it was a form of them, eternally pre-supposing them and never exhausting them. All that relates to being or quality (sense, impression) in reality belongs, considered per se, to the alogical. It represents the inchoateness of the first two elements of the conscious synthesis abstracted from the thought-form, which completes and gives it its final reality. Time and space Kant truly characterised as forms of sensibility; in other words, as forms of the alogical, thought (the category) pre-supposed them, just as they presuppose the primordial »I,« which is at once nothing and all things, nothing per se and all things per synthesis. So with the content of time. This also belongs to the alogical; its thatness, its being, is but the »I« of the original conscious synthesis re-appearing on another plane; its whatness, its quality, is but the »feltness« of the second moment of the synthesis. The category or thought-form, the »I think,« is only the reciprocal relation, and thereby the actualising of the as yet merely potential elements of »I« and »feltness.« To employ the term (» thought,« »idea,« Logos) which specially signifies this completing or actualising of the synthesis for the synthesis in its totality, or as concrete, can only lead to confusion. The distinction may be conceived as one between the potential and the actual.

If reality, objectivity, experience, consciousness-in-general, concreteness, according as we choose to term it, be a synthesis, it may be said that in the process of analysis it disappears, and that, therefore, any such analysis can serve no purpose. But all that philosophy does is to distinguish in thought, i.e., by the aid of reflection or thought on the psychological plane, those elements of which thought is the issue and, therefore, which thought presupposes. It would, of course, be quite illegitimate to treat them as themselves »real« or as »kinds« or as »things«; or again to conceive the so-called transcendental process as a time-process, as having a before and after. The synthesis as analysed in reflection, as sundered into its elements by thought, inevitably wears the garb of time. But this is an unavoidable illusion of the logical faculty which is accustomed to function under the form of time. Of course, with a separation (were such a thing possible) of its transcendental component momenta, reality or the concrete would be dissolved. But this is the case not only with the metaphysical synthesis of the consciousness, or with reality in its most comprehensive sense, but also with the physical syntheses or realities which occur within it. Thus the material synthesis, life, presupposes certain chemical elements; it is nothing but these elements, but yet they exist as a biological reality, as living, only in their synthesis. Dissolve this synthesis, and the reality, »life« or »living thing,« has disappeared. The synthesis is immediate. The elements in abstraction are there, but not the thing, the concrete itself.[3] The difference, of course, is that although in the dissolution of the organic synthesis, the reality, life, has disappeared, yet another material reality, an inorganic concrete, chemical substance, still remains; whereas, with a hypothetical dissolution of the ultimate synthesis of all reality – the supreme synthesis of the consciousness – no concrete would remain over. There is no other plane from which its component momenta can be viewed, every act of apprehension involving this synthesis. But, as before said, all that philosophy pretends to do is to distinguish these momenta in their concreteness. From the primary synthesis of the consciousness, which every definite consciousness presupposes, philosophy deduces its method, This method is known as dialectics. Its procedure is to tear out the process which constitutes the essential in every plane of existence or in every real by discovering therein the same contradiction and the same resolution of that contradiction into a higher reality as is involved in the original bare fact of world-apprehension. This key it finds will unlock the innermost secret of every reality, in psychology, in physics, in biology, in anthropology. Its category is action and reaction, the reciprocal cancelling of each other by contradictory elements. In this it differs from the standpoint of common-sense, the »classical« category of which is »substance and accident,« as also from that of science, whose favourite (though not exclusive) category is »cause and effect.« Philosophy qua philosophy deals in every case with the elements of concretes, rather than with concretes themselves. Just as it contemplates knowledge or consciousness-in-general in the making, so it regards all departments of »reality« according to the absolute conditions of their possibility, rather than according to the phenomena as presented in their concreteness. The Hegelians of the »left« thought they could retain the method of dialectics apart from metaphysics. But the dialectical method without metaphysic is a tree cut away from its roots. It has no basis and therefore no justification as an instrument of research. Unless we recognise the fact, that thought enters into the constitution of reality, that reality is nothing other than experience possible and actual, and that the unity of experience and the rationality which we find in the universe, or the system of experience, is deducible in the last resort from the primal unity of the consciousness, and from the condition of its synthesis – unless we recognise this, where is our locus standi in employing the dialectical method? Or in fact, where is our ground for assuming a determinate order in things at all? The commonest categories must then be inadmissible, and we have no alternative but the Humean position in its most extreme and impossible form.

The obvious and oft-repeated truth – so obvious, that it only requires to be stated to be seen by the most uninitiated – to wit, that the sum of the collocations of matter and motion, which we term Nature or the external world, is simply a system of categorised sensations, and that to gratuitously assume non-sensuous, uncategorised things-in-themselves as existing some-where or other behind »phenomena,« is a meaningless absurdity, of itself suffices to dispose of the theory of the cruder materialism. Every fool nowadays knows, or ought to know, that all psychical facts or phenomena may be interpreted in terms of matter and motion, and so far every man with any pretension to culture is a materialist. But this leaves the metaphysical problem precisely where it was before, matter and motion themselves being simply general terms for sensation differentiated and synthesised by thought, and apprehended by the Ego. All that the above materialism really means, is that on the empirical plane – i.e., on the assumption of experience in general as already given in its concreteness – mind presupposes material conditions, or otherwise put, this particular mind existing here and now, is dependent on, and subsists by virtue of, a material structure, to wit, an organic body of which it is, in a sense, the function. The individual mind necessarily presupposes the whole conditions of experience as given. But the object of metaphysic is to inquire how they come to be given; what is involved in this synthesis of which the individual mind is, and on which it feeds? The result shows us that the »matter« and »mind« of the vulgar are neither of them ultimate, but alike owe their reality to their apprehension or apprehensibility, which, again, merely means that they are in the last sense the self-determinations or functions (objects) of an »I.« This alone constitutes the possibility of abstract thought – »matter« and »mind« having a common basis. Because of this, we recognise the »law« reproduced in our minds as identical with the law imbedded in the »object.« We perceive the object itself, indeed, simply, because at bottom »it is of such stuff« as we are made of, its nature being perceptibility or apprehensibility. It was Hegel himself, I think, who started the mot, »The real is rational, and the rational is real.« But true though this is, it is sometimes used to give colour to the fallacy before alluded to, which Hegel, with certain qualifications, champions, that the real is all rational. A completely rational or logical world, a world resolvable into

181

pure thought-categories would at once cease to be a world, as a very little reflection will suffice to show. Reality we find is compounded of reason and non-reason, of logic and the alogical. Each by itself is abstract, but both alike are modes of Iness, and involved therein, and in this alone they are concrete or real.

The theory of Panlogism in its strict sense is reflected in the popular theistic notion that there is no such thing as chance in the world. If there were no such thing as chance there would be no such thing as law. Law and chance, necessity and contingence, representing the logical and the alogical in the dynamic of Nature, are mutually complementary. The individual or particular in Nature, as such, is always irrational; it is the domain of chance. As given in reality, of course, every concrete particular has a universal or logical element, but the element of particularity in it is always warring with and confounding the logical element, the unreason resisting the reason (see Handbook of the History of Philosophy, 2nd Edition, appendix). Time and space, as the forms of the sensible or particular, in other words, of feeling and of feltness, are the hunting-grounds of chance. The »sensible« always tends to infinite plurality, just as the »intelligible« always tends to definite unity.

Among the vain attempts of reflective thought to reduce chance to law, or rather to extract a logical rule from what is essentially alogical, may be instanced the »theory of probabilities« in mathematics, and, indeed, more or less the whole science of mathematics. The free-will controversy affords another instance of the abortive attempt to discern a rule in chance, to extract logic from the alogical. For will per se, mere nisus, is nothing but a form of the »I« more fundamental, as Schopenhauer rightly saw, than the logical principle and presupposed by the logical. The fixation of the relation between the »I« and the first form of the object, namely, the »feltness« in which it negates itself, in other words, the most elementary form of the synthesis of knowledge, involves this nisus. It is, therefore, prior in nature to thought, and belongs to the »I« or alogical principle per se. The individual, psychological will, inasmuch as it operates through consciousness, follows motives given, but its true nature, as Schopenhauer well says, »shows through;« it is known immediately as inness, and hence the impossibility of fitting it into the logical category of »cause and effect« – the category of mediateness or outness par excellence. On the mechanical plane, the plane of pure outwardness, all things follow the law of causation, all things are mediate, but it is not so here. Will is not pure determination from outside, from something not itself, it is self-determined, although it is easy enough when viewed from the outside to bring its phenomenon under the law of causation. As we have before pointed out, every concrete, every reality, as such, has an alogical and a logical, a sensible and an intelligible side: it is only a question of which is dominant. When we take our standpoint in the particular, we have to do primarily with sensibility, unreason, chance; when we take our standpoint on the universal, we have to do primarily with thought, law, intelligence. The particular of common-sense (so-called) or of ordinary perception, is, of course, a particularity already synthesised, although imperfectly, by thought. The »world« of common-sense nevertheless is a world in which particularity and unreason dominates. Science by means of the categories of reflective thought distinguishes the thought-element in common-sense reality from that of mere blind particularity or being (sense-element), and reconstructs the sense-world on an amended pattern. Philosophy shows the categories of science to be inadequate, as having the particularity of being or of sense still cleaving to them. It reconstructs the world of common-sense experience and of scientific thought by the light of those principles which all experience presupposes, after having traced them up to their highest source in the primitive synthesis of the consciousness. Thus in philosophy is reproduced, or rather indicated, in the forms of reflective thought, the core of the

183

process of all reality.

If my analysis, as briefly outlined in the foregoing, be correct, we may trace, as already said, in the dialectical process which at once interpenetrates and embraces all reality, a double alogical element underlying the logical. Thus in ordinary »presentment,« or »perception,« we have the apprehending, feeling, »I,« negated in the form »feltness« (all perceiving is a sinking of the »I« in the object), reasserting itself as thinking – assigning to the »feltness« its own attribute – self-subsistence (being), but as over against itself; imparting to whatness a thatness – in other words, we have the synthesis subject-object. In ordinary perception, the play of thought-categories in the object defining and limiting, hides the element of mere apprehension, of pure aesthetics. Only on one plane of knowledge is thought-activity subordinated to the passivity of apprehension, of feltness, and that is in the art-consciousness. In the special form of contemplation implied in absorption in a work of art, which constitutes esthetic enjoyment, we have a suggestion of uncategorised »feltness,« in so far that the work of art, as such, abstracts from, and throws our consciousness into, a condition of abstraction from the antithesis of the one and the many – an antithesis wrought by that re-assertion of itself by the »I,« as thinking, over against itself as mere »feltness,« which is the first condition of concrete consciousness. Art has an ideal, in the sense of a presentative, content for which time, space, and the categories sink to the level of mere accidents. The demand (so to speak) of the »I« to find its own activity (thought) in its other self, in its limitation as »feltness,« is stilled. The »feltness,« the presentment, is not as in ordinary consciousness subordinated to the forms of thought. But here the content has an immediate meaning which we term beauty, and which (pace Burke, Shaftesbury, Hutchison, etc.) is untranslatable into the essentially mediate terms of the logical.

Let us sum up now in a few words the practical importance of philosophy in general research. Firstly, it indicates the method to which all reality conforms, and Which is its highest formula. The presentation of the dialectic of any plane of knowledge is the most comprehensive expression of its law, its supreme explanation. This method again shows us that the most developed category is that of reciprocity, or action and reaction, rather than that of cause and effect, and that in the last resort all reality turns upon this category. The relation of reciprocity can obviously only obtain between the elements or momenta of wholes or concretes, and not between wholes or concretes themselves as such, for it implies that the one element is as essential to the whole as the other, and that, therefore, the whole can only exist in so far as they maintain their interconnexion. For example, it is sometimes said that on the assumption of a law in history individual effort in the interests of progress would be useless; for if the individual is a product of economic and other surroundings, and if every event is determined by pre-existing conditions, individual initiation must be excluded. But the mistake here is in confounding a relation of reciprocity with one of cause. The fact that the economic conditions of an age mould the men of an age does not exclude the fact that men react on economic conditions. Each factor is inseparable from the other. History, or human development, is a self-contained and highly-involved synthesis, and as such, its salient category is »action and reaction.« Though there be a distinct law of economic and social development which affirms itself in the long run irrespective of individuals, this does not by any means render the exertions of the individual of no avail, for the following reason: The logic of human evolution, like the logic of every other synthesis throughout all reality, is in a sense independent of time and space, which latter fall primarily to the sphere of the sensuous, i.e., the alogical. Every logical process (assuming it to be correctly stated) must realise itself somewhere and somewhen, but the where and the when are undetermined. Now the determination of this where and when is a matter of chance, of unreason. The individual, this individual here and now, who, qua the totality of history, is a mere chance product[4], or any number of such individuals may therefore empirically determine this a priori undetermined fact, for they are working in their own element. The logical processes of social development, as of every other development (biological, for example), in so far as they are embodied in the time series as concrete, may be arrested or delayed at any stage. They must, of course, assert themselves in their completeness at some time or other, but not necessarily at any particular time or in any particular case. Individuals, as such, may therefore very easily accelerate or retard indefinitely the course of progress (since they are working in their own element, that of chance), in spite of the fact that progress is in the last resort logically determined in its main outlines. Intimately connected with the above is the fallacy at the root of the denial of any general law in history, on the ground of the chaotic character of the phenomena of history. Owing to the great complexity of the content of human society, history appears like a frothing sea, without law or aim. For instance, that the whole Greece-Roman civilisation passes away, giving place to a state of society resembling the Homeric in many important respects, and that the development has to begin over again, so to say, seems irreconcilable with any logical process until we reflect that this is merely an illustration of the struggle ever renewed of the logical to assert itself, to realise itself in the alogical.

The reason of the shrinking of philosophers from recognising the alogical (sense, being, etc.), as one of the momenta in reality is the consciousness which reflection, or discursive thought, the first-born of the logical, forces upon us that its own moment thought ought to absorb sense and being, that the real ought to be rational and nothing but rational. This conviction seems confirmed by the fact that the logical is always encroaching on the alogical, both in the physical and the psychical spheres, that mere blind being ever recedes before thought, chance before law, impulse before deliberation. But it is forgotten that this absorption of being by thought is only approximative and relative. Every sphere of being comes more and more under the sway of the logical – law invades the realm of chance. But yet the dark background of sense-quality and of mere subsistence still remains – thought never becomes thing, reason never absorbs feeling completely. Thought brings to light endless processes in reality, but there is the thatness and the whatness of reality which thought glances off. They remain immediate in consciousness and its abstracted form thought, the mediating principle, can never express them. This is the kernel of truth in the hackneyed and often abused phrase of mysticism respecting the inadequacy of thought and words to express our deepest experiences. »Feltness,« qua, feltness, can never be rendered in thought or a fortiori in words – we cannot explain what being is, nor expound what feeling feels. This also, as already pointed out, is the real meaning of art, which suggests a perception as far as possible removed from discursive thought. Reason, analysis, categorisation, is the antithesis of the art-consciousness. The very word aesthetic which is used to express it, indicates its essentially non-logical character. Only in philosophy where the abstraction of thought is carried out to its furthest limits does it transcend itself, and by enabling us to regard experience as an articulated whole, reveal itself as essential to that whole, yet as a derivative rather than an ultimate element. But if thought, or reason – the principle of definition, of formulation, of relation, in short – is not ultimate, but implies certain momenta in their nature infinite, it follows that the notion of finality in philosophy must be given up. Philosophy must be no longer regarded, as Hegel regarded it, as a closed circle, but rather as an endless spiral – a progressive conception becoming, it is true, more and more adequate to its content, but never furnishing a solution of the world-problem in a formula valid for all time. The basis of the conception remains the same, but its statement varies, and must vary from age to age. We cannot affirm, indeed, that the thought-forms or categories which go to make our present experience, the reality of our present consciousness, may not be superseded at an indefinitely later stage of time-development, or at least lose that leading position which they have now; just as our »world« must be a different world from that furnished by the consciousness – assuming such to be – of lower forms of life.

Philosophy, then, is the final pronouncement of thought on the great problem of life, reality, experience. If it is destructive it is also constructive. It is thought holding up to itself the mirror of reality, recognising itself therein, and also its opposite, the not-itself, its shadow, which it implies and without which it would have no meaning. It is also the science which furnishes us with the method to which the subject-matter of all other sciences in the last resort conforms. In the infancy and childhood of society, man vaguely felt his oneness with the world. The mythological and magical theory of Nature universal with primitive man, is the expression of this vague half-consciousness. Man has not begun to distinguish between self and not-self in abstract thought. Reflection has not attained to consciousness with him. He does not reflect in the strict sense of the word. He feels the substance of himself and things to be one and the same, hence fetishism and totemism. All things live like himself. But no sooner does reflection arise, no sooner does he acquire the power of Abstract thought, and his consciousness become definite, than the world and himself fall apart. Every department of experience splits up into two mutually opposing sides. Man is now as mind opposed to matter. Later on precision is given to this view and he becomes subject (in the psychological sense) as opposed to object. His soul is opposed to his body, just as God is opposed to the world. Science accentuates these antitheses. It necessarily adopts a one-sided materialism as opposed to theology and philosophy (which is as yet theology's handmaid), and which found themselves on an impossible spiritualism or an abstract idealism, only varied by a dualism which unites the absurdities of both standpoints.

Everything is here viewed under the category of cause and effect. But reflection itself forces us at length to recognise the insufficiency of these standpoints themselves, the products of reflection though they are, and points out the standpoint of the future to be a return to Monism, not the unreflective Monism of primitive man, but a consciously reasoned recognition of the metaphysical unity in difference, in reciprocity, of all things, inasmuch as all that is real is the object, the thought-feeling, the determination, of the basal element »I.«

E. Belfort Bax

Notes

1. The word reality is used throughout this article in its current philosophical connotation as synonymous with the synthesis of the concrete, and not as by Kant, and occasionally by more recent thinkers, as denoting the special element of quality or feeling within that synthesis, abstracted from the synthesis as a whole.

2. A good instance of Hegel's attempt and failure to reduce what is per se alogical from the logical is his treatment of space and time, the leading points in which are to be found in the Encyclopidie (Ed. Rosenkranz, pp.208-219).

3. Thus the specific real or synthesis, human society, may be conceived as disappearing, while its mere material, the human animal, remains over. Evolution consists, of course, in the resolution or disappearance of one real synthesis into another, which we term higher as opposed to its resolution into its elements, which we term dissolution. But in evolution the general synthesis of the logical universum remains in its concreteness as the basal element through all its forms – e.g., medieval society disappears, its reality is gone just as thoroughly as in dissolution, but the general synthesis, society, remains realising itself in other forms.

4. I may here make the general observation that a sum of contingencies can never give necessity. One can trace back the chain of antecedents of a particular event, but each link is determined by something which might have happened otherwise.

189

11. Note on "Now"

From Outlooks from the New Standpoint, pp.199-203.

WHAT is now? The negation of the past and of the future. It is the point at which time vanishes. Time is duration. But now, the present, has no duration. It, therefore, does not exist in time. Again it is impossible to conceive time otherwise than as infinite, i.e., we cannot conceive a time before which is no time, yet it is evident that if now is in time, time cannot be infinite, since if an infinite time has preceded now, now could never have been reached. Yet again, the time which succeeds now can never be infinite, since it has had a beginning in now. So far, therefore, as time with its one dimension of infinite length or duration is concerned, now is distinctly "out of it," for now has no length, no duration. What, then, is now? Let us consider this now more narrowly. If we do, the first thing that strikes us is that now is the inseparable attribute of I. The actuality of I we may say is identical with nowness. I am and now are at bottom three words signifying one thing. All nowness is the form of I-ness, and all I-ness is the being of nowness. In itself now like I can never be seized. The now which is a definite thought – an object – is not the true now at all, but the conscious moment just left behind. In the same way the I which we think of when we say myself – which is object to us – is not the true I, the I that is thinking, but merely a pseudo-I, a synthesis of thoughts and feelings reflected in this I which are immediately or intuitively identified with that I, but which on analysis are distinguishable as such. This synthesis, moreover, in so far as its content is concerned, discloses itself not merely as distinguishable from the true outlooking, thinking I, but as accruing to it only by accident. Similarly the pseudo-now or past moment of consciousness, which is a definite thought and which is a part of, or, indeed, the foundation of time, is also identified intuitively with the true now which it presupposes. This identification again has to yield to the results of philosophic reflection. The I that thinks is not the I that is thought of, and the now that is present in consciousness and as a part of time is not the now that presents that present to consciousness.

We see, therefore, that the presenting now, though it must necessarily involve the content of the presented now, does so only implicitly. This first becomes explicit or actualised (as phenomenon) in the presented or pseudo-now which constitutes the minimum possible of time and which hence may be regarded as the unit of time. Its content is nothing other than the thinking, outlooking I itself. Reality or experience is, therefore, the actualising or explicating of I-now. I-now in its true sense is impersonal, undifferentiated, potential. It is always rushing into time-consciousness, but yet is never exhausted in time-consciousness – always remaining behind as the infinite possibility or potentiality of consciousness. This potentiality is reflected in the plane of concrete experience or Reality itself as the being or substantiality of things in contradistinction to their mere appearance or actuality. For this distinction is in the last resort traceable to that between the I-now, which thinks and presents, and the thing thought considered per se, that which is thought and presented in it. From one point of view, the thinking and presenting I-now may be regarded as the material, and the thought and presented, as the formal moment in the primal synthesis of reality, or concrete consciousness. Now is the eternal transition from the potential to the actual. But from another point of view, or rather more narrowly viewed, the now is always formal, and it is the I which constitutes its material content. This has already been indicated above. The filling of now is I-ness in the infinity of its determinations which we term sense. The categories or thought-forms which constitute the other factor in experience are, as Kant, with true philosophic instinct, saw, deducible from time, which is in its turn deducible from the timeless now, termed by Kant, the "Synthetic unity of apperception." This is the form of sensibility from which rather than primarily from the Begriff or logical moment, as Hegel insisted, the universe of thought and things is reconstructable.

Kant truly saw that the logical itself presupposes the presented now or unit of time, although his psychological prepossessions prevented him seeing that the content of the logical, the thing-in-itself which the sense-phenomenon presupposed, was nothing other than the Ego or Subject to which alone the phrase "in-itself" can with any significance be applied. The in-itselfness which Kant saw behind the sense-impression was of course merely the projected in-itselfness of the Ego. But the further and more serious result of this mistake was that Kant separated the "unity of apperception," the formal now from the I of which it is the form, and after attempting to deduce the fundamental thought-categories from this "now," or so-called "synthetic unity," (an attempt of course in itself perfectly justified even if the execution was not very successful), fetched the material element from outside without attempting to incorporate it in his deduction. He thought to make an impossible separation between "Metaphysic" and "Theory of Knowledge." No metaphysic is worth anything that is not based on a Theory of Knowledge; but, on the other hand, no "Theory of Knowledge" is complete or accurate that does not embrace a metaphysic. The one without the other is a barren abstraction. To get over this difficulty Kant had to separate sensibility from thought proper. His system therefore fell asunder into a dualism. His successors from Fichte to Hegel seized upon the formal side of his doctrine and built thereupon the theory of the exclusive dominance of the concept or completed formal activity – thought. (See Handbook of History of Philosophy, 2nd edition.)

But another and hardly less important blunder of Kant was his making time to be exclusively a form of sensibility. That space is a mode of sensibility alone is obvious,but it is surely scarcely less obvious that time is more than this, being in addition the mode of the formative or active principle of consciousness, deducible from the "synthetic unity of apperception," or, as I have termed it, the true now. We get rid of Kant's difficulty when we recollect that actuality or thought is merely a function or rather the resultant of a function of the I, of that which thinks, that its mode is time deducible from the timeless now. It is the thought-form now that sunders or negates the I, that fixes it and thereby dualises it into I and not-I, which in the last resort is nothing more than possible and actual consciousness. The subject, or I, is always the possible, the not-I, its shadow, always the actual.

Will, I take it, is the nisus of this transition, of the realising of the I, in the concrete or real world, or, in other words, on the time-plane. The transcendental act of self-realisation, the fixing of the I in now is reproduced in the empirical sphere as will. Will is the tendency of the Ego to realise itself. But what shall we call will? The best definition of will I can find is "the infinite imperfection of thought." Perfect thought casts out will. Will may be termed the dynamic of thought, thought the static of will. Will by nature exhausts itself in an act, in a "real" synthesis, which is its object. When once this is attained, will as such is abolished. Could we therefore assume à la T.H. Green, a completed actuality of thought – an actual thought-synthesis which has exhausted all possibility of thought – we should arrive at a will-less God in a timeless Now. Such a synthesis is of course absurd, as it excludes the conditions of a synthesis – it would be a form without matter, an actual without content. But if we grant it, such is its nature. For now as such, always represents completeness. Will in its transcendental source as the becoming the fixation of the I, as consciousness, is necessarily abolished in

193

the completed moment of the fixation or arrestment, i.e., in the Now. Hence the Now is the negation of Will. We see this illustrated (I may observe in conclusion) in the empirical sphere, in the distinction made between Nature, the fixed order of realised consciousness, the synthesis of all nows, and Freedom, or the lawless element of will which we regard as the power of originating events in time without reference to natural causation.

THE END